To,

From the author

M000189225

# MY PLAYMATES WERE ESKIMOS

*David Greist*

## DAVID GREIST

### EDITED BY ELIZABETH A. COOK

For Copies write:

DAVID M. GREIST, USAF, RET.
2079 Kingswood Ave.
Deltona, Florida 32725

CHICAGO SPECTRUM PRESS
LOUISVILLE, KENTUCKY 40207

CHICAGO SPECTRUM PRESS
4824 BROWNSBORO CENTER
LOUISVILLE, KENTUCKY 40207
502-899-1919

Printed in the U.S.A.

10 9 8 7 6 5 4 3 2 1

ISBN: 1-58374-043-0

This book is affectionately dedicated to Alicia, my wife of over 50 years (now deceased), who, with Nelson Alsup, encouraged me to write these events.

I am very fortunate to have had Elizabeth Cook as my editor. She has been a student of Iñupiat (Eskimo) culture and language for a dozen years. She shares a love for the Arctic and its people equal to mine. The background information and introduction which she has written are a result of extensive research on her part. My sincere thanks and grateful recognition to her for her advice and help.

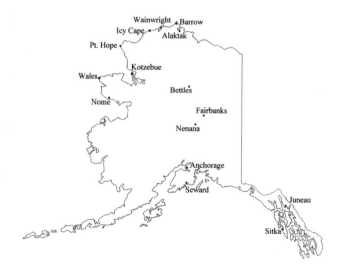

# CONTENTS

# PREFACE

*The following is a compilation of stories, profiles, observations, and commentary from David Greist's boyhood, much of which was spent in Barrow, Alaska. David's childhood, from 1920 to the early 1930s, parallels a pivotal time in the history of Alaska's North Slope—long after rifles had come and commercial whaling had gone, as reindeer herding had moderate importance, but while fur trapping was changing the economic landscape of the region.*

*Growing up among Iñupiat Eskimos in an arctic coastal village that was home to fewer than 500 people, David held an advantageous position from which to recall the recent past of the region. His parents, Mollie and Henry Greist, were missionary members of a very small white population within an entirely native community and he was the only white child in Barrow for many years. His bicultural upbringing and lengthy residence through a formative age allow him to muse on life from several diverse perspectives. As a child growing up under very different circumstances than his white peers elsewhere, he is able to reflect upon American culture as he viewed it through his narrow filter. It was only the other white people in the village and the bits of mainstream American culture which arrived on a boat once per summer, that taught him all that he knew about the white outside world until his first outing to the lower 48 states in 1925.*

*On the other side of consideration, however, David's bicultural position lent him a glimpse into Iñupiat life very different from that of his parents. Surrounded by Iñupiat buddies, girlfriends, co-workers, and siblings-by-proxy, he spoke the Iñupiaq language, ate the food, accepted the customs and, consequently, came to understand the culture at a level unattainable by many. Although he lived and worked within the confines of his Midwestern-styled home and his parents' hospital and church, much of his time was spent on his own, doing what Iñupiat boys did—hunting, playing, tending his dogs, and performing the chores necessitated by life in the Arctic. He heartily experienced both sides of his world.*

## ABOUT THE EDITOR AND THE PROJECT

*As an undergraduate student at Indiana University I became acquainted with the Greists and their lives through my own work at the University's Mathers Museum of World Cultures. Fascinated by arctic culture from a very early age, I traded the delusional life I lead as a child—after reading* My First Book of Eskimos *at the age of five, I was convinced that I was an Eskimo—for the study of Iñupiat culture via a BA in cultural anthropology.*

*As a student cataloger at the Museum, I worked with the extensive collection of material accumulated by the Greists and later deposited there. Initially intrigued by the vast array of objects in the collection, I was soon in awe of the story behind the collection, the life the Greists had lead during their 17 years in Barrow and elsewhere in Alaska. Each member of the family had an elaborate and fascinating story. Henry Wireman Greist, a physician living near Indianapolis, had always wanted to go on a mission. After marrying Mollie Ward Greist late in life and turning down the opportunity once at her insistence, he jumped at a second offer for an assignment by the Presbyterian Home Mission Society. Mollie Greist, dedicated mother, daughter, and nurse, painfully left the Midwest to serve beside her husband in parts unknown. She agonized over the last time she would see her aging parents and worried about the welfare of the child she would raise in this undetermined life. David, a child of two, was thrust into the adventure of his life and dumped into another world, for which he would have no comparison for years to come. As it turned out, he was to grow and thrive in an arctic desert.*

*While performing research for my master's degree at the University of Alaska-Fairbanks, I had the opportunity to make three trips to Barrow to interview elders who had been children with David. Although I sought information about David's parents for my project, the women lit up when they spoke about David. Everyone had a story to tell of boyhood mischief or sisterly torment. Everyone also had the overwhelming reaction that he was as close to being Iñupiat as a non-Eskimo could be. I had the pleasure of speaking with Terza Ungarook Hopson, a woman with whom David spent a great deal of time when they were children. When asked about David, the first words out of her mouth were, "He was one of us, you know." As she elaborated it was clear that, to them, he had never been merely the white child who lived at the Presbyterian manse. And she was not alone in her response. As I spoke with other elders, I met similar perspectives. In their eyes, he had spent his childhood as just another kid— a brother and a buddy.*

*I became acquainted with David Greist during a visit to Orlando, Florida in 1995. Knowing he lived there, I packed photos and questions, tapes and recorder, and called to invite myself into his life. He and his wife, Alicia, graciously invited me to their home. I told him about my vicarious interest in his life, attempting to make my presence legitimate, and the stories began. We reviewed pictures. We talked about his childhood and his parents. We discussed contemporary Barrow. I left them having been educated and enchanted by the lively stories they conveyed about the Greists and life during and after his family's time in Barrow.*

*Early in 1996, I was overjoyed to receive a phone call from the Greists, having been recommended for this project by mentors in the life history/oral history field. After considering the stories David had to tell and collecting more than a few on paper, David and Alicia sought an editor to collaborate the tales and supply the history and culture necessary to make the experience meaningful to an outside audience. Together we embarked on this process, David wrote stories about specific events and I created narrative that would tie those stories together. Following the third draft and the sudden death of Alicia in 1997, the project took the form you see here—alive and loved and thoughtful. We all sincerely hope you enjoy the stories.*

*The stories contained in this volume are a combination of oral accounts given from the author to the editor and written accounts created by the author in isolation. Throughout the volume, the reader will see plain type entries that are first-person accounts written by the author, David Greist. Additionally there are passages in italicized typeface which are the words of the editor, Elizabeth Cook. Historical and cultural information has been employed where needed to clarify a point and references have been made to works both contemporary with the author's childhood and reflective of more recent research.*

# INTRODUCTION
# MY PARENTS & THEIR MISSION

First some background information of Barrow and our family. I am David Greist, the son of Dr. and Mrs. Henry W. Greist formerly of Indiana. Dad was a medical doctor and a doctor of theology and Mother a registered nurse. Both were very active in the medical profession in Indiana. I was the only issue from their marriage; my mother was 45 at the time of my birth. The doctors in Indiana diagnosed her as having a tumor; I was eventually that tumor.

In 1920 Dad and Mother were offered positions as medical missionaries to arctic Alaska. Dad, an ordained minister of the Presbyterian Church, had always wanted

*We terminate 17 years in the Artic, August, 1936.*

to go as a missionary to a foreign field and they gladly accepted the assignment to Alaska.[1] Dad was 52 and Mother 47; I was 2. We lived in Nenana, Juneau and Fairbanks for some two or three years, however, most of my childhood was spent in the Arctic. The language I learned was Eskimo. I played and hunted with the Eskimo. I learned to run dogs, the main means of travel by natives and whites at the time. I met my first white boy living in Barrow, son of the local schoolteacher, when I was 13 years old. He did not like hunting, dogs or Eskimos.

I think Mother and Dad were both dedicated and they accepted the Eskimos for what they were. Dad didn't want to change too many of their customs except those that would benefit their health like ventilation in their homes and maybe hanging up a curtain between the parents and children so the children couldn't watch the mother and father during their sex acts, things like that. He tried to get them to bury their dead instead of putting them on top of the ground and to not feed their babies walrus flipper. He was against their dancing and was kind of adamant about that. I didn't see anything wrong with their Eskimo dances, but he thought there was something too pagan about them. He was strict about that and ended up writing some disparaging things about the dances. Now card games, he couldn't do anything about that. The Eskimos loved to play cards. Overall though, he loved the Eskimos. When he and Mother left Barrow everyone gathered around the ship. He said they were singing hymns and everybody was crying. He loved the Eskimos and hated to leave them.

*As for anyone in that time when few moved to the far north, the transition to the Arctic made by the Greists was a long and intentional one. Although Dr. Greist relished the adventure, having wanted to take the assignment 5 years before, Mrs. Greist expressed great trepidation about the trip and the idea of leaving her elderly father and friends. She feared a future of raising her only surviving child[2] in the*

*Arctic, so isolated and far away from all things safe and familiar. In her memoir,* Nursing Under the North Star, *Mrs. Greist lamented, "I had to promise that I would go, but I could not promise myself that I would go... with tears in my heart and eyes dropping on the thousands of different articles I was packing I still hoped that something would happen to stop it all."* (Greist 1967:2)

*When the Greists arrived in Alaska, they surely had no idea of the journey on which they were embarking. At that time, missionaries were expected to stay for no more than 4 years and then be furloughed or permanently replaced. The Greists spent 17 years in and out of the Arctic from 1920 to 1936—raising their son, practicing their medicine, and professing their Christianity. They could not have foreseen the impact they would have on the tiny community nor the changes which would occur during that critical time in Barrow's history.*

*During the 19th century missionaries from various denominations were vying to claim their chunk of Alaskan land and the disperse and large number of native souls which would be shown the ways of Christianity. In the amicable agreement that was reached by the represented denominations, the Presbyterians claimed a portion of northern Alaska, including Wales, Wainwright, and Barrow with influence over the Iñupiat population east to the Canadian border. Additionally Presbyterian influence spread south through the interior of the state, with outposts south to Nenana, Fairbanks and Seward, and along the inside passage of Southeast Alaska.*

*Although the history of the Presbyterian Church in Alaska reaches back to the 1870s, the first missionary, a teacher named Leander M. Stevenson, arrived in Barrow in 1890. A mission structure was built in 1894, designed to be a "chapel-school house and teacher's house combined."* (Report 1895:49) *By 1895, there were eight Presbyterian-sponsored schools across the state attended by 431 pupils. The Utqeagvik Presbyterian Church was organized in 1899 and was the only church serving the village until the mid-20th century. Horatio R. Marsh, the first medical missionary, arrived in 1896.*

*The Presbyterian Church's Board of Home Missions, first active around 1802, became responsible for the provisions of not only spiritual salvation but also social and medical welfare in the north. Although the Greists began as merely the next recruits in a long line of medical service to the North Slope, they were the first to be placed in charge of the new hospital there. Their mission of religious, social and medical assistance was an institution of wide influence as well as huge relief.*

## CAPE PRINCE OF WALES

*In the summer of 1920, Doctor, Mollie and tiny David Greist set off from Seattle on the steamship* Victoria. *They arrived in Nome for a 3 week stay before continuing on to Wales, a village that reaches out into the Bering Sea.*

Prior to our arrival in Barrow, my parents' first assignment was to stay a year in Wales, about 175 miles north of Nome some 90 miles from East Cape, Siberia.[3] Dad and Mother were able to get passage on a very small ship called *The Silver Waves* and, according to my mother, it was well named as it not only waved, it wobbled, rolled, and dipped. *The Silver Waves* traveled only from Nome to Kotzebue, which is the next village north of Wales. As related by my mother:

"My whole trip on this small ship was one continuous rock-a-bye with all my clothes on during those four days and nights. There was no convenience whatsoever. I was so sea sick the entire trip that Dr. Greist looked after me. David, age two, was turned over to the sailors.[4] What they fed him I do not know. Someone made a harness for him and he was tied with a rope to prevent him from going overboard.

*Dad converted this old trading post into a home for us.*

"On the fourth day we arrived at Wales. There were no docks. There was no ladder or basket to lower me to the waiting boat. The big captain just picked me up in his big strong arms and dropped me into the arms of a similar, big man, an Eskimo. Another of my dreams of Alaska washed away. My Eskimo was big laughing and kind. There were nine of them and they passed me from one to another until I was in the back of the boat. I looked up just in time to see my David coming through the air, his bottom as bare as the day he was born. I called to the captain to please pass down the diapers. He called back that there were no diapers. All had gotten dirty and were thrown overboard.

"I was greatly relieved to hold him in my arms once more. My heart and eyes were full of tears, to see that ship leave. I felt it was like the breaking of the bond between me and my home far away. Oh, why did I come! Those stocky strong men were smiling, mouths full of white teeth, heavy black straight hair, deep lines on their faces. Could these be the Eskimos of my dreams?

"The boat was scraping the sand on the shore now. Again I was picked up like a babe, my feet set on the sandy shore. A whole circle of 15 to 20 women with babies on their backs and children hiding behind them were staring at me, not a white face among them. I held David tight by his rope harness. I felt so lonely in this barren waste. Hot tears were burning my cheeks. I could not speak to them. I did not know their language. To my surprise a woman with a wonderful smile on her face came from the crowd, laid a hand on my shoulder and said in perfectly good English, 'Do not cry. We will not hurt you. We will help you.' She must have known what I felt. This woman was Lucy, wife of the native school teacher. I shall never forget it. Here, I was the missionary and yet I was being administered to by an Eskimo. Lucy took charge of David and harness and my tears were drying. She led me up to the school house with all the natives following."

Mother, Dad and I stayed with the school teacher after our arrival in Wales.

The first missionary to Wales was Reverend Mr. Harrison R. Thornton of West Virginia. He built a very fine home in Wales out of California redwood. It was a house of several rooms, thoroughly well built and well insulated. The once beautiful carpet had become moldy from age and dampness. There were pictures on the wall and cut glass and Haviland dishes were in an oak china closet of Mrs. Thornton's.

A young Eskimo man had murdered Mr. Thornton by shooting him in the back with a rifle.[5] A bride of only 3 weeks, Mrs. Thornton left everything behind in her haste to leave. All of these many years the natives never entered or stole anything from that house.[6]

My father could not use this home because it now stood within 3 feet of a precipice, the once wider premises having broken off with the sea pounding upon rocks 60 feet below.

With ax, hammers and wrecking bars Dad and an Eskimo, Lewis Tungwenok dismantled this goodly residence and loaded the same on their backs, carrying the materials to the former trading post building that was to be our new home. Dad, with the help of Lewis and Arthur Nagozruk used this material to rebuild the post, making it into our home. This building had not been used as living quarters since 1896. Travelers had used it as a dog house. Natives had stored seal, walrus, and polar bear meat in it. Quoting my mother, "It was the worst looking building I had ever seen." However, the location was desirable.

It took three Eskimo women and Mother 3 days to scrape the blood, meat and dung from the floor, only to find cracks in the boards half an inch wide in some places. In September we moved in with a bed for me and one for my parents. A hot water tank made from an empty oil drum was connected to the coal burning range.

The last boat arrived with our trunks, but without the 25 tons of coal that were to keep us warm. Dad was worried; he talked to the natives. There was no wood to be had. He talked little and prayed much. The teacher let us have 2 hods of coal a day, pending the arrival of our coal. This was sufficient to maintain the kitchen range for heat and cooking. The coal should have been on the beach in July, but our 25 tons of coal was on the shore at Nome.

When Ira Rank, captain of the *Trader,* sailed into Nome for the last time after his annual trading trip to Barrow, he had arranged to have his two-masted schooner pulled up on the beach for the winter. On the shore he saw this coal, 100 pounds a sack, all piled up. "Whose coal is this?" he asked. The man in charge of the dock replied, "It belongs to that fool missionary at Wales." "I'll be," said Ira, "He will freeze to death without this coal. I'll take my limit back to him." The dock man cussed, calling him all sorts of names for risking his boat for that missionary. This made Ira angry, so he had his first mate load 15 tons on the ship, which was the boat's capacity, and sailed for Wales.

He knew that the last boat was out from the Bering Strait for the winter.

You can imagine the joy and jubilation of my parents and the natives when Ira Rank's boat anchored off-shore. The natives wasted no time in long shoring the coal from the boat to the manse in their large skin boats. Ira would not accept any pay for bringing the coal. "If you are a fool for coming to this God forsaken coast to help these poor people, then I'm a bigger fool for risking my entire investment. I did it and I would do it again. Your God was with me during yesterday's storm. The devil tried mighty hard to send us to Davy Jones Locker." Ira was a tough little man, a man of the North who could out cuss the best of them, but his heart was larger than his body.

That winter, the 15 tons used sparingly, kept us warm. Arrangements were made to have the remaining ten tons delivered the next summer. But the real warmth of course, came from the people in this new strange place.

*The following year, the Board of Home Missions offered the Greists the post in Barrow and, although they had settled into life in Wales, they went. When the Greists arrived in Barrow they found a village with a new hospital, a well-established trading post run by Charles Brower, and many frame houses.[7] The mission complex was well constructed with a large, white steepled church and a two-story manse reminiscent of a New England whaling captain's home. There was a school, first established by the Presbyterians but since turned over to the federal government, which attempted to westernize the community's children as it taught them English and other curriculum from the lower 48 states.*

*At the time of the Greists' arrival, the Iñupiat people living in Barrow already had a long history of contact with whalers, missionaries, and traders. Barrow's small population had weathered the whaling boom which had swelled in the late 19th century and ebbed by the 1910s. They had become accustomed to the goods supplied by the trading ships and trading posts owned by whalers turned proprietors. Trapping had become a way of life for all those wishing to advance their family's material wealth.*

*By 1932, toward the end of the Greists' tenure, Barrow was home to 350, nearly all Iñupiat with "but 15 whites in 100 miles."* (Greist 8/1932:31)

# CHAPTER ONE
# PEOPLE

As I recall, Eskimo children were well behaved. I never witnessed any type of corporal punishment such as paddling, etc. by parents. Children did not quarrel or fight among themselves. Eskimo boys hunted all day in the summer with bows and arrows the old men of the village had made for us. We hunted snipe, ducks, lemmings or tin cans. We also made slingshots similar to the type used by David against Goliath. With these we hurled stones far out into the Arctic Ocean.

I remember the Eskimo as people who did not steal from each other or from strangers.[8] They were hard workers and very dependable and they shared what they had with those who did not. They were known to go out of their way to welcome a stranger into their igloo. The visitor's dogs were fed, and the woman of the igloo repaired any furs that needed mending.

Do not misunderstand me, there were a very few natives who were lazy, indolent, slovenly and dishonest, but the entire village was aware of who they were and they were watched accordingly. For example, it was the custom that whoever helped in the killing of a bear, walrus, or seal would share in the meat. One day near Barrow two hunters succeeded in killing a bear. As they stood near their prey watching it in its last throes of death one of these "different" natives ran up and fired his rifle into the dying bear. Reluctantly he was given a share of the meat. The villagers avoided him after that.

Dad held religious classes for several boys which resulted in one, Roy Ahmaogak, passing the catechism exam. Dad recommended that Roy be ordained. Bert Panigeo, who only went through the eighth grade, translated most of the new testament into Iñupiaq and taught school in Barrow. Samuel Simmonds went to seminary in California, became ordained and returned to Wainwright as a Presbyterian minister to his own people. Several girls raised by my parents went on to high school in Sitka, Alaska, then to college in the States. Flossie George went away to school and then returned to teach children in Barrow's government school. Cornelia Phillips, a full-blooded Eskimo girl raised by my mother, went on to become a registered nurse. Others also pursued higher learning.

### MOTHER AND HER GIRLS
*Mollie Greist is still remembered for the influence she had on the lives of Barrow's young women during her tenure. Having birthed only male children, she seemed to find pleasure in the company of local young women. Additionally, due to the limited number of professional helpers who would have relieved the Greists, and with all of the mission work to be done on a daily basis, extra hands were a necessity. Mrs. Greist taught several young women the subtleties of patient care. She also employed girls as kitchen help and laundresses in the hospital and manse and placed David in the care of many a young girl as she tended to her nursing responsibilities.*

*Reportedly unlike other missionaries' wives, Mrs. Greist seemed to take an initiative to change the status quo for the girls under her tutelage, exuding her influence during the transition from girlhood to womanhood. She wanted more for her young helpers and she assisted in sending girls out of the village for high school and instruction in some wage profession. In* The Northern Cross, *a quarterly newsletter that the mission published for supporters, Mrs. Greist explained, "The girls are brought up with one idea of securing a hus-*

*Hospital staff, including my mother and Helen. Helen and Lee Suvlu are on the far right.*

*band advantageously as soon as they can after a proper age, wifehood and motherhood being their one great ambition. The only exceptions are the boys and girls sent by us to our great school at Sitka at the Sheldon Jackson School. These boys and girls prepare for teaching, nursing, etc.* " (Greist 8/1932:32)

Mother always had several teenage Eskimo girls helping out or living at our house. They learned how to cook, clean house, do the laundry, mend and sew skins and clothing, and they all learned to speak fluent English. When one of them got married, Mother would replace her with another young girl. There were Cornelia Phillips, Flossie George, Kate Brower, Terza Hopson, Julia Segevan, Greta Akpik, Hester Neakok, Ella Sakeagak, Cynthia Ahmaogak and others, whose names I can't recall.

Besides the domestic chores these girls all had an important part in raising and looking after me. I have been told by Cornelia and Kate that I made life difficult for them. For instance, there were no radios in Barrow. The manse had a Victrola that these girls played all day long. It operated via a spring that had to be wound up. I would take the crank and hide it thereby making the machine inoperative—no crank, no music. They would bribe me with candy and gum to tell where the crank was, but it didn't work. Finally they would tell Mother and then I had to produce the crank.

Mother spent most of her time at the hospital acting in the capacity as nurse. She was the only registered nurse in the Arctic for quite a while and, for many years, her salary was $50 per month. The girls she trained at the hospital became very efficient in caring for and meeting the needs of patients. They also helped in overcoming one big disadvantage, the language barrier. Mother knew no Eskimo so the girls were excellent interpreters.

## HELEN AND LEE

Perhaps the most outstanding Eskimo girl trained in the hospital technique was Helen Suvlu. Not yet 20 years old, she learned quickly. She knew the names of all the drugs and where they were located. She worked closely with my father conveying instructions to patients in Eskimo. Helen and Lee, her husband, were our best helpers. Helen, at age fifteen, was the first native to greet us in 1921 when we arrived on the US Revenue Cutter Bear to Barrow. I was three and without proper Eskimo attire; she made me my first spotted reindeer parka and boots soon after we arrived. Helen was such a vivacious and eager person that Mother took her into the hospital as a helper in the kitchen. She proved so quick and apt that she was transferred to bedside nursing. She spoke understandable English and was also an energetic and consistent church worker who never lost a chance to spread the gospel message. Mother and Dad trained Helen to work in surgery, in the clinic, drug room, and obstetrics of the hospital. Helen never seemed to tire and was the only native mother knew who could awaken at night at the least noise in the hospital. Later she married Lee and soon became the mother of two. She never took more than 3 days off to give birth to a baby and return to duty. Her children were raised in the hospital kitchen where they were very well behaved and no problem. Helen was conscientious and gave unlimited service to the sick in all emergencies. She was the official hospital interpreter for Dad and Mother. Even though her education had been largely neglected, and her ability to write and spell were poor, her familiarity with drugs, their names, and uses were remarkable. All Dad had to say was, "Helen, I need this drug or that drug." She had memorized them all and their location.

Lee became the hospital janitor and an excellent mechanic, his skills refined through his association with Stanley Morgan, the wireless radio operator. Lee maintained the Kohler electric power plant and the Fordson tractor. He took care of the heating system in the hospital, kept up the ice supply in the hospital kitchen, emptied wastes from the chemical toilets,[9] helped lift and move patients and filled requests from the cooks for various cuts of meat from the meat cellar.

Helen and Lee each received $60 per month plus room and board. They were able to save enough money in 5 years to order enough lumber from Seattle to build themselves a two-story house in Barrow. At that time their home was the second two-story house in the village. Helen and Lee remained with the hospital until my folks left Barrow in 1936. She came down with tuberculosis the second year after we left Barrow and died without the care of a nurse or doctor. How ironic that the woman who had dedicated herself to the care of others should die without benefit of the same care. By then the hospital had been taken over by the federal government and the doctors and nurses had not inherited the empathy for the natives that Mother and Dad had.[10]

## OUR JULIA

*As the sole nurse in the hospital for many years, Mrs. Greist could rely on Helen and others, but preferred to watch over her charges personally. Meanwhile, David and Dr. Greist continued to live in the manse with Mrs. Greist sporadically at home.*

*Hoping that the Board of Home Missions would send his wife relief, Dr. Greist wrote of how busy their duties left them. In the June 1930 issue of* The Northern Cross *he described,* "Mrs. Greist must remain in hospital even at night, not caring to absent herself from the very ill, not daring to leave her native helpers, however efficient, with the responsibility. With a telephone asked for, and with the coming of another trained nurse, Mrs. Greist can get away for rest and relaxation. The manse then will become our home." (Greist 6/1930:45)

*Julia Egayuak Segevan lived with the Greists as their house girl for six years.*

From 1930 to1933 Dad and I had to live more or less alone in the manse. Mother, as head nurse, had to stay in the hospital. Sometimes on weekends she'd come over and prepare us a good meal. She would bring Terza and Ella or Hester with her and clean the manse, change our sheets and do our laundry.

We had two spare bedrooms in the manse, so it was decided that we should have a permanent house girl and cook. Julia was raised at Point Barrow, 12 miles to the northeast at the very tip of Alaska. She could not speak English, was about 5 feet tall and was an energetic and tireless worker. Mother took her into the hospital and taught her how to cook, keep house, make bread, biscuits, and all the other domestic duties. Along with this training she learned English and one of the first sentences she learned to say to Mother was, "I want to go out!" meaning that she wanted to go out into the village and visit with friends. Mother would let her go if she had her work done, but she had to be back at 11:00 or something like that. It was the same for the girls in the hospital. They had to have all their work done, the kitchen cleaned up and so forth and they had to be back at a certain time, too. The natives liked to stay out late and sleep late.

When Julia was new to the hospital she was helping to wash dishes in the kitchen one day when she accidentally dropped a dish. Much to her surprise the dish hit the floor and broke into several pieces. She immediately dropped another and it did the same thing. In her home all they had were tin plates. Before she dropped the third dish Miss Lillian Bailey, the head housekeeper, stopped and explained the difference in dinner ware.

After she had been in the hospital a year, Mother assigned Julia to the manse where she did a super job taking care of Dad and me. By this time she spoke pretty good English and my father claimed that she could make biscuits that would melt in your mouth.

One day Julia and I were fighting or playing or something and I pushed her up against the gun rack. My finger must have hit a trigger because a 410 shotgun fired and spattered the front door with shot. Of course we didn't want Dad to know all this, so I think Lee helped us cover up all the holes with putty and paint over it. When we were up there in 1996, I showed the lady of the house where I shot the door.

## TERZA

*Terza Ungarook Hopson was another girl who spent a great amount of time at the mission. She worked in the house and in the hospital and was one of the girls who filled the role as David's surrogate sister.*

I roomed in the hospital for a time and there was a dining room where Miss Bailey, Dad, Mother, and I ate at a big round table. The hired help ate at a long table in the kitchen. One day we were having dinner and the dessert was apple pie. Terza said to be sure to tell her when Dad was about to eat it. So as the pie was being served I said in Eskimo, "It's being served. He's getting ready to eat it.

He's eating it now." Dad looked up and asked in his normally stern voice, "Who made this pie?" We said that Terza had and he said, "Terza, this is good pie!" She was very surprised, very pleased.

One day at the hospital I wanted to go to Browers' because I was going with Maria, one of the Brower daughters, at the time. I had several chores to do and I asked Terza to help me. I said, "If you help me, you can go with me over to Browerville and I'll carry you across that little creek."[11] She said, "Oh, okay," and helped me, doing some of my chores. While she was doing one of them, I took off. She later said that she looked out the window and said, "There goes David down to the station without me." She never got over that.

## MARIA

At the age of seventeen I had been interested in Maria Brower. We had been dating for about a year—she was beautiful. I went to Mr. Brower one day while he was taking off his boots in his bedroom. "Maria and I want to get married," I said. "It's all right with me," he said, "but have you asked your father?"

The next day I did. That summer I was sent to Stony Brook School for Boys, a Christian boarding school in New York. I was there 4 years. The romance cooled and we stopped corresponding. Years later Maria married a fine Eskimo, Joseph, with whom she had nine children.

## MY FRIEND WOODROW

*Although girls predominated the crowd that spent time at the manse and hospital, David made male friends, too. It is through this male companionship with Clyde, Bartlett, Benjamin, Walton, Furst, Eddie and others that David learned skills typical to any boy on the North Slope. With them he would hunt and travel, work with his dogteam, and trap. His attachment to this idyllic boyhood scene ended, however, when he was shipped out to be schooled in the lower 48. Stony*

*My chums (l to r): Clyde, me, Woodrow, and Bartlett.*

*Brook School for Boys was a far cry, both socially and proximally from Barrow.*

For several years Woodrow Isaiah Okakok was my Eskimo chum. He was among the several Eskimo friends who taught me arctic survival skills. We went hunting and traveling together, played ball and went on various short trips on the motorcycle. He was 4 years older and one of the strongest guys in Barrow. One time, in a contest, he carried five sacks of coal 20 feet, each sack weighing 80-100 pounds. He had one under each arm and three on his back.

One day Woodrow and I decided to put both of our dog teams together, pulling one sled. Well, when we got through, we had a team of twenty-one dogs, probably the longest in Alaska. There was a serious problem, however. My team wanted to fight Woodrow's team. It was all we could do to keep them separated. The idea failed and we drove a half mile across the frozen lagoon, turned around and went back to my home. We had quite an audience of spectators, however. We had never seen this plan attempted before.

Woodrow, another friend Walton Ahmaogak, and I would go seal hunting in the fall or in the spring. We ate seal liver; seal liver is excellent. We'd use the rest for dog food. Sometimes the seals would have a hole in the ice and you could sit there and wait for them to come up, but you had to have a lot of patience to do that. The Eskimos would sit on their little work sleds and when the seals came up to breathe, you know, that was it.[12]

On several occasions Woodrow and I went up the Arctic coast hunting eggs for my mother.[13] We spent a week or so and collected eggs and birds and nests. Marvin Peter would help blow the eggs and wrap them very carefully in cotton, tying them with thread and packing them very carefully to be sent to museums. Usually all the ambulatory patients helped, did their share of the work around there. Mother kept them busy.

Woodrow and I corresponded while I attended Stony Brook. He died from tuberculosis in 1936, after my folks left Barrow.

## MARVIN PETER

Twelve miles northeast of Barrow, was the settlement of Point Barrow with only eight to ten igloos and just a handful of people. My father preached there each Sunday afternoon, beginning when he was assigned the mission at Barrow.

Ida Gordon Numnik, who was from the Point, worked at the hospital in Barrow and told Mother that she had a brother there who could not walk. Mother and Dad were both interested. Dad had never seen Marvin on his feet at the Sunday afternoon service and thought nothing of it.

Through an interpreter he learned that Marvin had been paralyzed since he was a very small child. By then he was 18 years old, had never had any schooling, and had never walked. His legs were flexed at the knees; he always sat on them.

He consented to an examination and Dad told Marvin that he was not paralyzed, but that he had had inflammatory rheumatism when very young. Dad told him that if he would come to the hospital for a year, he would straighten his legs. By following the method prescribed by Dad, Marvin Peter was walking all over the village on crutches within 18 months. The process was painful, however. He was lifted bodily and sat in a large tub of warm water, made hotter gradually for an hour. Then Lee, the janitor, would lift him into bed and the nurses would rub and massage those legs until he cried, "Enough." This was done twice a day for weeks until his legs began to loosen up. Helen Suvlu and I would take turns massaging him five or six times between baths. It was not long until Marvin was observed doing the massaging himself.

All those years, while sitting on his legs, Marvin made tools for the hunters, bone needles and steel needles for the women's sewing machines, dog harnesses, parts for lamps, and seal and fish nets, repaired traps and typewriters and lashed sleds. Knitting was an art with him. He crocheted and cut quilt pieces perfectly for Mother. He hooked rugs better than my mother could. He could draw anything he looked at. He expertly skinned birds, ducks and geese and blew eggs for my mother's collection for the ornithologist. Many of the items he made are now in museums in Chicago, Indianapolis, and Bloomington, Indiana.

I have a movie of Marvin on his crutches and also a whale bone basket he made for me. I have a pair of gloves he knitted with my name woven into them. They could easily be mistaken for machine-produced gloves as his skill and precision were so great. During his last years he was given a job in the Barrow school teaching the children all the skills he had been using all of his life.

*Marvin Peter became a renowned baleen basket maker[14] and community photographer. Noted by Molly Lee in* Baleen Basketry of the North Alaskan Eskimo, *Peter had a 33-*

*year basket making career, manufacturing over 500 pieces* (Lee 1983). *Being crippled and extremely sedentary as a child, Peter spent many hours working with his hands. His artistic talent flourished and he was able to master all the craft skills that were taught to the girls in Mrs. Greist's craft classes as well as those needed by men preparing equipment for the hunt—a hunt he had no opportunity to participate in until a young man.*

*Additionally, Peter was a prolific photographer, documenting the people and activities of mid-twentieth century Barrow through hundreds of images. The legacy left behind by Peter and his camera is still heralded as a treasure for the North Slope and the Barrow community. He comprehensively documented events and individuals previously only recorded sporadically by passers-through.*

*His talents, however, did not stop with baleen and film, he was ever-present around the Greist home during the mid-1930's and helped as needed with sewing, knitting and other projects. He would participate in projects to create gloves and socks for local people at Christmas time. On his accomplishments Dr. Greist commented, "Marvin is a genius at knitting, and does some remarkably artistic work. He now goes anywhere on crutches. However, he is never idle, but carves ivory, weaves wonderful baskets from whalebone, and with yarn can make your eyes glisten."* (Greist 1/1934:51)

## REX

I remember Rex Ahvakana, a teenage Eskimo peer of mine, who learned radio and Morse code from the army wireless operator Sergeant Stanley Morgan. He wanted to learn music and Dr. Newell, a predecessor of my father, was a pianist and taught Rex how to read music and play the pump organ. Rex was our church organist for 12 years. David, another of the Brower children, had a piano at his house and sometimes Rex would play that. We'd all go over there and listen to him play the piano.

## Mr. Hopson

*Unlike the Greists, Fred Hopson was a member of the white community who, upon his arrival, made Barrow his permanent home, taking a native wife and raising a family. As Charles Brower's right hand man, he held a prominent position in Barrow society.*

Mr. Hopson was a friend of Mr. Brower's and was his cook for a while. Mr. Brower's family got so big he asked Fred to be his cook, to help take care of them. He worked in that big kitchen in the back of Mr. Brower's trading post and fed the whole family back there.

Mr. Hopson went to Barrow in the late 1800s with Mr. Brower as part of a whaling crew. He was father to Alfred, Steve, Ellen and another boy. Mr. Hopson was a photographer, too. He had a little old-fashioned camera and took some good pictures.

## Women at the Mission

*Over the years of the their service in Barrow, various women traveled north to assist the Greists. Some came as personal friends and others as nurses. While the extent of their presence is poorly documented, their company and help was surely greatly appreciated.*

Florence Dakin was head nurse from 1921 to 1929. To me Miss Dakin seemed to be a very arrogant, very domineering woman. She didn't ever trust my father and ruled that place with an iron hand. That frustrated him. When we moved back in 1929, Mother became the head nurse. Miss Dakin ultimately died outside Alaska from tuberculosis.

Miss Ann Bannon was the housekeeper for the manse and church in the 1920s. She was then sent to Saint Lawrence Island and Cape Prince of Wales. She had to do first aid and she was always asking Dad, "Doctor, what can I do in a case like this?" or "'Can you send me some simple medicines I can use?"

Augusta Mueller was a young nurse from New York who served with the mission beginning in 1922. She was trained in anesthesia.

*Miss Lillian Bailey, a friend of the Greists from Monticello, Indiana, was also a staff member at the mission. Lill, as Mrs. Greist referred to her, helped out at the manse and hospital for a time as a housekeeper from 1929 to 1933. She was also a Sunday School teacher.*

*Evelyn Komedal came to be a nurse in Barrow from the Aleutian Islands. She arrived in 1931 and left in 1933 due to ill health. While in Barrow she helped with the Junior Society of Christians.*

## DOCTOR WAUGH

Dr. Waugh was an orthodontist from New York City, a very wealthy and successful dentist. He would go up on the ship *Northland* and visit the villages along the coast where he would check on teeth and do whatever he could to relieve pain. He was also a photographer and he had camera equipment and a tripod and he would have one of the sailors carry that for him when he came ashore. He would work on teeth and then go take pictures. I talked and visited with him in New York when I was at Stony Brook. I was up in his office and he showed me all of his pictures and everything. He made some beautiful pictures; he was a good photographer.

*Dr. Waugh left behind some stunning photographs of his time in the Arctic. Although David had the opportunity to accompany Dr. Waugh to Labrador during a summer when he attended Stony Brook School for Boys, David instead returned to Barrow. He was drawn home to help his parents pack for their last trip out of Alaska.*

## THE MORGANS

In the late 1920s the Army sent Sergeant and Mrs. Stanley Morgan to Barrow with their daughter Beverly who was 10 years old when we went back in 1929. Beverly became my shadow and wore all my hand me downs. I never did see her in a dress. We hunted together, played and drove dog teams together. She was a regular tomboy. One Christmas Mr. Ford, our scientist houseguest, and I gave her, not a shirt or new pair of blue jeans, but a .22 rifle. We were inseparable buddies until I was sent to the States for high school when I was sixteen.

The Morgans lived in the little house that we lived in after the manse burned for quite a while until the government built them that house on the point. Her father had operated his wireless radio outfit in that little shack. He was an officer with the Army Signal Corps which had operators in different parts of the world. They received and transmitted messages for their communities and reported any unusual activities. It was all done by Morse code; there was no talking. He could stand there and talk to you and send his message. He was real good.

Just for something to do one day I decided that Beverly and I should take all my dogs in the house to see how they'd behave. They went completely wild; they'd never been in a house before. They knocked things over and we got them outside real quick. After that we tried to straighten up the house and put everything back the way it was. We never did that again.

There was one other white kid, the son of the schoolteacher. Our relationship was short-lived. He was about my age, but he did not like hunting, dog teams, or trapping and couldn't speak Eskimo. He and I did not become compatible, so it was just Beverly, our Eskimo friends and me.

## For Mothers Only

One day at our public school in Barrow where my mother was a substitute as a teacher she noticed that several youngsters would don their parkas and run home. An hour later they returned. She asked Bert Panigeo, a native teacher, why they did that. "Mrs. Greist, they go home to nurse." "What! you mean they are still breast feeding!"

"Oh yes," said Bert.

One day a mother brought her small baby to our hospital. She told Dad, "Baby, he weak, no grow." After examination Dad determined that the baby was starving to death. Through an interpreter Dad learned that this mother had nine other children with the two youngest still nursing. Dad insisted that the mother put the two other children on canned milk and nurse the baby, otherwise the baby would die. The mother of the infant complied with Dad's orders and the baby survived. According to my mother that particular mother had not been dry for 30 years.

Eskimo mothers carry their babies on their backs under the warm deer skin parkas. Mother was curious as to why the babies never wet on their mothers' backs. Through, Helen, interpreting for Mother, this is what transpired:

"Did you never use diapers on your babies?"

"No," said Helen.

"Why?" asked Mother.

"Because they are dirty and smell bad," replied Helen.

"Well," Mother asked, "what do you do when the baby is on your back?"

They all laughed, "Baby let us know."

"How?"

"Oh, he squirm a little, we take him off and hold him on the snow and he make water quick."

"And the other?"

"The same."

"How do you clean him?"

Helen answered, "Maybe a piece of calico in summer, in winter a piece of snow."

Mother then asked, "Why do the women carry a coffee can hanging from their belt in church?"

"They do not want to take baby out on snow while Dr. Greist is preaching. They let the baby down from their backs under one arm after they unbuckle the strap, and hold the baby on can in their laps after he nurses and then set the can on the floor under their chairs."

A mother with a brand new baby would spend the first 10 to 12 hours nursing her baby and holding it on a can or tin cup every 15 to 20 minutes until she got the first urination. After that she had no trouble for as soon as the baby squirmed she put it on the cup. This she continued night and day until the baby would not urinate unless it felt the cup on its bottom.

*Mollie Greist surrounded herself with local mothers during her time in Barrow. Her Mothers and Better Babies Club changed the ways Iñupiat women approached caring for their children and keeping their households. Gathering various women of the village, she founded the organization in 1921 and, according to an account in* The Northern Cross *of March 1936, "lectured as to the sanitation and the proper care of the little ones, that care beginning nine months ere birth and extending not until the next child arrives but until well on towards maturity." The girls and mothers met for instruction and discussion and regular baths for children and laundry sessions for mothers were held.*

# CHAPTER THREE
# NORTHERN BOYHOOD

*Although David Greist was a unique entity among his peers, he was considered by many of his friends as one of their own—socially, intellectually, and culturally. During the days he would play with his peers, living an Eskimo boyhood and speaking fluent Iñupiaq. At night he would return to his Midwestern-style home where his parents exercised the mores of any lower 48 minister's family.*

## ESKIMO INFLUENCE

During my early years at Barrow, my toys consisted of my dogs, sled, bow and arrows, kites, and rifle. My Barrow playmates were all Eskimo until Beverly Morgan arrived. Naturally, I ate Eskimo food and learned to speak their language. Often when I came home from play, I would forget and start jabbering to my mother in Eskimo.

When I was a young child, Mother insisted on nap time for me. Native kids didn't take naps, but I had to. From 2:00 to 4:00 p.m. each afternoon I was subdued and confined to a bed by my mother after much screaming, kicking and crying. At these times Mother noticed that several children would stand and sit outside on the snow. She went out one day and asked what they wanted. "Oh, we're waiting for David to come and play."

At an early age I learned to respect the animals of the Arctic and their preservation. Eskimos do not kill for the excitement of it or kill just to be killing. Everything they killed was eaten and the skins used to make garments. The

700 to 1,000 dogs of the village had to be fed. The meat of seals, whale, polar bear and walrus was considered adequate dog food. Nothing was wasted.

Whenever a stranger arrived in the village by dogteam all the natives would vie with each other to make the stranger a guest in their house. He would be given the warmest place in the house to place his sleeping bag. His dogs would be unharnessed, tethered and fed. Food was cooked for him and hot tea, in the only cup with a handle, was his. Then the family would stay up way past midnight pumping the stranger for all the news from where he came. I have been told that whenever a native came to our house in Barrow, I would immediately offer him food and water.

Lee and Helen Suvlu were responsible for my Eskimo name. We were out goose hunting behind Barrow about 30-40 miles away. I noticed some dog tracks in the snow and I called Helen's attention to them.

"David, those are wolf tracks. Don't you know the difference between dog tracks and wolf tracks?" they asked and laughed, "From now on your Eskimo name is Amaguq which is Eskimo for wolf." I still can't tell the difference between dog and wolf tracks.

Lee taught me how to tie knots, how to drive the mission's tractor and how to cut the select sections of meat from frozen reindeer carcasses. He also took me goose hunting, taught me how to call the geese and how to knock them down with a 12-gauge shotgun. My training and introduction to Arctic survival and living was from my Eskimo peers.

## My Birthday Party

Eskimo children did not celebrate birthdays when I was a boy. When I was five my mother decided to have a birthday party for me with my Eskimo playmates. This is how my mother recorded the event.

"David was five and had made many friends with the Eskimo boys. He was tall for his age and a leader always, now old enough and brave enough to roam all over the village. He talked their language and played their games.

"This was March 31st when the sun was shining more than 8 hours a day. The snow was hard and the temperature -30 degrees. David and his friends played games in the house and outside.

"I saw Elder Bert Panigeo and hired him to bring his big dogteam and sled and take the boys for a ride. They all piled in and Bert took them down the sled trail out of sight of the village—something not often experienced by children of this age unless, of course, accompanied by their parents.

"According to Bert, the boys howled and screamed. They sang songs throughout the 8 mile round trip and when all came back two native girls, Cornelia and Kate, and I had set a long table with decorations, candles, little favors at each plate, and birthday napkins. Kate and Cornelia had helped me make cake and cookies, peanut butter sandwiches, pumpkin pie, popcorn balls, nuts, candies, and chewing gum. There was milk and ice cream with chocolate syrup. The children had never experienced anything like this. They were thrilled to take home their favors.

"It was at this time that David was tired of having his curly head combed and set by my fingers every day. It was decided that the curls would be cut off. He would then comb his hair like his daddy. As I remember there were five of us for the operation. Daddy held his hands and talked to him. Cornelia and Kate and I received the curls and our favorite Eskimo barber operated. David was afraid it would hurt.

"The curls were sent to grandmother Greist in Indiana. Because of only four first class mails each year we did not know that she had passed away one month earlier. I am sure that David does not remember any of this."

## A TYPICAL DAY FOR ME

*As might any son in Indiana, David was expected to do his share of work around the mission and, as he grew into a tall, strong boy, his share increased accordingly.*

Everyday I had chores to do in the morning. I would clean out all the ashes from all the stoves, chop up kindling for the next morning's fire, and fill all the coal buckets with coal and bring them in. I would go out and get ice, clean it off and put it in the big tanks in the kitchen so that it would melt for drinking water. Then I would go out to the meat cellar and cut up any meat Julia wanted for dinner or supper the next day. If Dad had some work for me to do with Lee at the hospital then I would do that. After all this I would feed my dogs. If the coal room was empty I'd have to go down to the coal house with the tractor and bring coal and fill it up. That would all take a while to do. All this took up most of the day and in the evening we would listen to the phonograph or play games at the hospital, things like that. Sometimes we would go over to Brower's store where he had a pool table and we'd play pool—Sadie, Maria and some of the others. That was about it.

My Eskimo friends didn't have the chores I did. Their lives were really simple, confined to one room really. I don't think they did the things I did. They were always ready to play ball though and go hunting or walking or things like that. They would come over to the house all ready to play, but I had to get all my work done before I could go out.

The day started at about 9:00. Dad was up early, before anyone else. He would build the fires, get the kitchen fire going and get it warm in there. Then he would get Julia and me up. By then he would already have made something to drink and Julia would make our breakfast, usually oatmeal and toast, things like that.

And in the evening after everything was finished, he'd always have a Robert Burns cigar after supper. They were kept in the storeroom and I'd go out and get it for him when he was ready for his cigar.

## MY FIRST RIFLE

An Eskimo boy learns early to shoot a bow and arrow and becomes an expert in the use of the sling shot. I also was given a bow made from hickory, from Jim Simigluak, with several arrows each tipped with the empty brass cartridge of .25-20 or .30-30 caliber ammunition.

We hunted phalarope and snipe in the summer. We did not shoot at sparrows or snow birds because they were not edible, however the breasts of the phalarope and snipe were delicious when baked by my mother. We had to have ten to fifteen of them to make a good dinner.

After a boy became proficient in the use of a bow, usually at 13 or 14 years of age, his father would present him with a .22 rifle. With the rifle he was given five cartridges and told, "Son, bring back five birds and the rifle is yours." If he only brought back four, then the rifle was taken and put away for 7 days. The procedure was followed again with five cartridges. This time you can be sure that he was extremely careful and accurate in hunting. When he brought back five birds, he became the proud owner of the Winchester .22. From then on he helped supply meat for his family.

When I was twelve, after he had taught me how to shoot, my father gave me a Stevens single shot .22 rifle. Soon after, my father wrote to his sister in Indianapolis:

"David is in his element with wild duck, snipe and phalarope. He killed four ducks in one day with his .22 rifle, eight snipe and I know not what else. He keeps the snipe until he gets enough and then the young people have a fry. He had sixteen for the feast one day last week. These eight are a starter towards another feed.

"He is now very tall, as tall as his mother, but slim as a rail. Shoes and boots I bought last summer are too small.

A suit I got for him from Indianapolis, a $25 affair, is outgrown."

Sergeant Morgan had a .12 gauge Remington pump shotgun, which he kindly let me borrow for king eider ducks, geese and brant hunting. For ducks and geese I used shotgun shells with number 4 shot. Large flocks of king eider ducks made their way north along the coast opposite Barrow. My buddy Woodrow and I would go out on the frozen sea ice and hide behind an ice cake. We would see the ducks coming half a mile away because the sky would be black with hundreds in each flock. We would wait until they flew past and then fire into the flocks as they flew away from us. Their feathers were so thick that the shot could not penetrate and kill them, but as they flew past the shot could go up under the feathers. Woodrow and I often knocked down eight or nine each time they passed over and in 3 hours we had all the ducks we could carry home. Woodrow was a much better shot than I.

The brass shotgun shell was very popular. It was cheaper to load your own brass shell and, in the early days, we filled our brass shells over and over again. We had a regular loading kit. You put in so much powder, and so much shot and use the rod to press it down, then turn it over and put your primer in. Later they had the regular shotgun shells made out of pressed cardboard. Those came from Winchester and used number 4 shot for geese and ducks. Charlie Brower's wife loaded all her own shells. She was a good shotgun woman. She would take two of her little children with her and they would run out and pick up the ducks after she shot them down.

Duck season would start when they started to migrate in the spring and, of course, everybody went out hunting them. You'd hear shots out all over the ice and then we'd go inland in the spring for geese and so forth. In the summer time would be plover, because the plover would come up all the way from South America to nest. Dad and I went out behind the church one time and shot twenty-two of them. They're very good eating. Then there are the ptarmigan. They were good eating too, but they were hard to see in the winter time. I also shot an owl one time, but you can't eat those.

### TRAPPING FOR THE FUR

*As the commercial whaling industry left arctic waters, various men chose to stay behind to work in the Arctic as traders, satisfying the Iñupiat's acquired taste for western goods. In order to support this hunger for trading post merchandise, fur trapping became widespread. Trappers would leave the village during the winter months and go out on the trap line hoping to capture arctic fox. They would collect those pelts and trade them at the trading post or on board one of the annual ships as they sailed by in the summer. Men, couples, and whole families would live the trapping life. Missionaries frowned upon the lifestyle, wishing for families to stay closer to the village so that their children could go to school and their families attend church. Still, the draw of the migratory life and the value placed on fox, wolverine and wolf skins by the outside market, caused many to continue trapping and, if necessary, leave their families for extended periods of time to do so.*

*Growing up as any Iñupiat boy might have, David learned the ways of eking a living out of the tundra. Although he was destined not to live his life in the Arctic, he felt an affinity to the landscape and the culture surrounding him and consequently absorbed the lessons of adulthood as his friends did. So avid was his enthusiasm for trapping that, in* The Northern Cross *of January 1931 at the age of twelve, he wrote to announce the beginning of trapping season and to discuss his first adventure.*

*"The trapping season opened December 1st. On the 8th I got out my two traps, or the two I had found when walking upon the tundra last summer, that had been lost by someone and I cleaned them up. Being the first time I ever went trapping, I went three-quarters of a mile inland, a very short*

*distance.*" (Greist 1/1931:21) *Additionally, he described the process he had learned. Although his father taught him how to shoot, he learned about trapping from Iñupiat friends.*

During my early years at Barrow, fur trading was the primary economy of the Arctic and income for the Eskimo. Greenbacks and silver coins were non-existent. The only economic concern for an Eskimo was how much flour, sugar, tea, coffee, ammunition or calico one could get for a white fox skin at the trading post. For many years, Charles Brower had the only trading post at Barrow. During the 1930s the going price for a good white fox was $60. This would enable a native to get a Winchester .30-30 rifle and three boxes of cartridges.

I was thirteen when I first started trapping. My first traps were set south and in view of the village. They were so close to the houses that I never caught a fox, but I had lots of practice setting the traps. As I became more experienced, I would travel by dog team inland for some 20 or 30 miles, one day's journey, and set up a base camp. My base camp was a large snow house where I stashed my sleeping bag, food and gear. From this camp I would start out in the morning, making a circle circuit via a loop.[15] Returning to base camp that evening, I would place a trap every 100 yards or so on this circuit.

Setting the trap was one of the arctic survival skills I learned from Lee Suvlu. First you had to select a place where the snow was firmly packed. You dug down with a snow knife—like a butcher's knife with a blade 10 inches long—about 5 inches deep and large enough to hold the trap.[16] The end of the 3 foot long chain was buried deep in the snow with a short stick attached and stomped hard with your boots. This 'dead man stake,' as it was called by Dad and the natives, soon became frozen and was very difficult to pull out.

You then carved a thin, pancake-like slice of snow. Very carefully you placed this over the opened jaws of the trap and then, with the knife, you scraped back and forth until the snow pancake was very thin. You then placed small pieces of meat around the trap and slowly covered your tracks as you backed away toward your sled. Mr. Fox would smell the bait, walk to the trap, step through the thin snow pancake and activate the trap which sprung shut on his leg.

During the trapping season, then from December 1st to March 15th, a person could set out 50 to 75 traps. Then each day you would leave your base camp and visit your trap line to retrieve any foxes caught. Trappers who stayed away from the village for the entire season could bring in 40 to 60 pelts.

When I was a boy, one of the most successful Eskimo trappers was a man called Taakpak who lived east of Barrow. It was not unusual for him to bag 100 to 200 foxes in a season.

On one occasion when Taakpak took many of his pelts to Captain Pederson on the MS Patterson, he said to Captain P', "I want to buy a dress for each woman in Barrow." On another occasion he asked Captain P' to bring him a motor boat with a cabin on it from San Francisco. I was on the *Patterson* the summer when the 30 foot boat was hoisted onto the deck of the *Patterson* and we delivered it to Taakpak at Barrow. Our ship's engineer went aboard the boat and gave instructions to Taakpak and his sons on operating the six-cylinder Kermath engine. Taakpak's boat was the envy of every native in the Arctic. It cost him at least 100 white foxes which then was $6,000 delivered.

Besides fox furs, Mr. Brower would give $1 per foot for polar bear skins. These skins were sent to the States where they were mounted as polar bear rugs. Reindeer hides, walrus and seal hides were not traded, as they were used by the Eskimos for garments, boots and coverings for kayaks and whaling boats or umiat.

## SALLY TAKES ME HOME

*Hunting for various birds, David did his share to fill the family's meat cellar. Frequently traveling with friends to shoot geese or other game birds, they would travel 30 miles inland and set up camp awaiting the migratory fowl or out toward Point Barrow (Nuvuk) to a hunting ground located at Pigniq referred to as Shooting Station. The trip was usually made by dog team and mushing became a favorite activity of David's.*

Although I had dogs as pets from the age of two, I began raising a dog team with my mother's help. They were all related to my leader Sally, who was the mother, grandmother, and great-grandmother of all nine of them. Sally was a very intelligent dog; she was part Greenland and part Siberian. I took Sally for a walk through the village one time and a loose dog came and started to attack me. Sally took care of him. He ran back home with his tail between his legs. She was the only dog I had that I could take on walks with me. As a puppy she was given to me by Jim Allen, a trader at Wainwright; had a very fine team of dogs.

When I was 16 years old I was given permission by my father to go trapping inland from Barrow. I loaded my sled with food supplies, rifle, sleeping bag etc., plus frozen seal meat for the dogs.[17] I headed inland to set traps for white fox.

I made camp 45 miles south of Barrow on the edge of a frozen lake. I built a 2 x 12-foot snow house using a snow knife, similar to a machete. I cut out 2 foot wide blocks 6 feet long and stood them up on end, each one touching, creating the walls. For the roof I cut the same size blocks and leaned them against each other on top of the walls creating a peaked roof. All of the cracks were filled with loose snow making the house air tight. When this process was finished I cut a small door in one end, large enough for me to crawl through.

Snow blocks are very light, easily cut and shaped. In my new home I placed my grub box, sleeping bag, extra furs, boots and mittens plus a small kerosene burning Primus stove.[18] The seal meat was also in my igloo to prevent the dogs from getting to it. My sleeping bag was made from reindeer skin and very warm.

This was my base camp. The next day I hitched the dogs to the sled and set out to set traps for fox. The sled was empty except for the traps. I set out my traps in a huge semi-circle two miles from camp. I had fifteen Victor steel traps and, after setting them out, I returned to my base camp in the evening, fed and tied the dogs and prepared my meal of heated frozen reindeer stew over the small Primus stove. I had to be careful not to heat up the igloo to the point when the ceiling would start to melt.[19] I would check the dogs one more time and then turn in. Sally slept in the igloo with me on a pad of her own. It was good to have something alive with me to dispel the loneliness.

During the night the wind increased in velocity. The next day I visited the traps and found one white fox. That evening the wind increased to gale force with blowing snow. The temperature went to -40 degrees. I was confined to the camp, the blizzard lasted three days. Each day I untied my dogs, fed them and dug out my sled. Everything was being buried by the snow: dogs, sled, and my snow house. After the third day my snow house was completely covered with snow. I walked over the top of it not knowing there was a house below me. I no longer tied up the dogs, knowing they would stay near the camp.[20] Several times during the day I would push my empty sled into the force of the wind for about 75 yards, turn it around, stand on the back with my arms out stretched, the wind would push me likity split across the snow towards the base camp. I would then step on the brake and repeat the process until I was tired. The dogs ran along side, they probably wondered why they were not in their harnesses pulling the sled. That, and reading some *Saturday Evening Posts*, helped me pass the time.

The entrance into my snow house was now a vertical tunnel 6 feet down with a 90 degree turn into the original opening of the house. I kept the tunnel free of snow everyday. I was able to lift Sally to the upper surface, she only weighed about 65 pounds. I heard later from Sergeant Morgan at the weather station in Barrow that the wind velocity during the storm was 56 miles per hour.

By the third day I had run out of people and dog food. On the fourth day I decided to go home. I hitched up the dogs, loaded the sled and headed home to Barrow. Visibility was reduced by blowing snow to where I could only see the first four dogs in front of the sled. Every 30 minutes or so I would stop the team and with my warm hands I would remove the frost and ice from the eyes and nostrils of each dog, and any ice from between their toes. When I saw drops of blood on the snow passing under the sled I knew then the dogs' feet were bleeding. I stopped the team and on each foot I tied a small canvas 'bootie'— something I learned from the natives—which was the size of a small bag used by children to keep marbles with a draw string. These 'booties' did the job; there was no more blood on the snow for the rest of the trip.

My lead dog, Sally, was nearly always unseen by me because of the blowing snow. I had no idea which direction we were going except I knew we had to travel with the wind, blowing at right angles to us from the right.[21] I trusted Sally to get us home. One of my dogs, Rusty, who had been pulling hard all day collapsed on the snow from lack of food and exhaustion. I stopped the team, unhitched Rusty from the main line, took him out of his harness and placed him on the sled. He lay there with his head thrust forward towards the team, I think I detected a smile on his face, this was a first for him. Sled dogs do not ride on sleds. He stayed on the sled the rest of the way home.

At about 6 p.m. the team suddenly made a 90 degree turn to the left. I stopped the team and made my way up to Sally. She had discovered a much used dog team trail running along the coast to Barrow. I went back to the sled, turned her loose to lead us on. Two hours later the team suddenly stopped. I again worked my way up to Sally and lo and behold there in front of her were the steps leading up to the manse. Sally had done it again. You can be sure that I fed the dogs a good meal of reindeer meat that evening. They were really 'dog' tired. They seemed very happy to be home, so was I.

The next day Julia wakened me with the remark, "Your mother wants you right away at the hospital!" I dressed and went over and found my mother. "David," she said, "do you know what happened to the two large trays of reindeer meat we were going to make stew out of for the patients?" "Yes," I replied and I told her the whole story. She was sympathetic, but also displeased. "Please, don't do that again, I had to find something else to feed everybody today."

## A TRIP BY DOGTEAM

One March, while planning a trip to Wainwright, 110 miles down the coast, I made the following preparations. Planning to make the trip in three days, I used nine dogs with Sally as the leader. A week before our departure I checked all the dog harnesses. Any that were in need of repair I took to Julia, our house girl, cook and housekeeper and sweet-talked her into fixing them for me. I checked the sled and made certain that there were no screws missing holding the steel plates onto the hickory runners.

I cooked and browned bite size pieces of reindeer meat and made a stew with canned vegetables and fresh potatoes, if we still had any from the supply that came in August. The finished stew was poured into flat pans to the thickness of about three-quarters of an inch and placed in the outside store room which was unheated. The stuff froze

*Part of my team with Dad's sled, summer 1934. Returning from the post office with sacks of first class mail.*

hard in just a few hours. I would then break it up into small pieces like peanut brittle and put it in a clean, empty flour sack. My meals for the entire trip consisted of this stew and other miscellaneous food items.

I cleaned my .30-30 Winchester rifle and removed any oil with gasoline. At 30 to 50 below zero, oil in moving parts congeals thus sometimes preventing the firing of the rifle. The gun was carried in a seal skin case strapped to the side of the sled for easy access.

My Primus stove, made in Sweden, was checked and I carried two in case one failed. They burn kerosene and were the main source of heat and cooking that we used in the Arctic. I carried 2 gallons of kerosene on my sled in metal containers. Several pairs of wool socks, a sewing kit with skin needles, sinew, and thimble were always a must for any traveler in the Arctic. Should you tear your boot on a sharp piece of ice you were expected to repair it yourself. All Eskimo men were properly instructed by their wives on the art of repairing skin garments. So was I.

A hand saw and large knife similar to a machete were part of my equipment. These items were used in building my snow shelter each night. An ax was carried to chop up seal meat for the dogs. My sleeping bag was made from reindeer skins with the hair on the inside. I would not undress on the trip except to remove my parka and boots.

On the day of the journey, Julia filled two Stanley thermos bottles with hot cocoa—all other travelers usually had hot coffee, but I did not begin drinking coffee until I was 45. The thermos bottles were encased in their individual reindeer bags which, of course, helped to keep the liquids hot in sub-zero temperatures.

I dressed in cotton long johns (I couldn't stand wool), two pairs of blue jeans, four pairs of socks, two wool long sleeve shirts and, of course, my heavy fur parka and fur boots. I wore two pairs of canvas gloves inside large fur mittens that were fastened to lines around my neck. If I had to untangle a dog's harness, I could slip my fur mitten off and I thus do the task before me with my hands in canvas. When my fingers got cold I put on my fur mittens again.

Woodrow was my frequent travel companion. When my hands would get cold, and my gloves frozen stiff, he would trade with me. His gloves were toasty warm and, in about 30 minutes, we'd trade back and he would have my gloves soft and warm. We would do that all day long. Probably being a white person, not an Eskimo, I always had difficulty keeping my nose and fingers from freezing. Eskimo noses are flat. Mine sticks way out into the elements. I kept warming my nose with my bare hands or I'd turn my head a quarter of a turn into my fur head piece so that my nose could get warmed up against the fur. There was no problem with my feet; the colder it got, the more socks I put on.

The sled was made ready by placing a canvas cover over the sled with all duffel and equipment placed inside. Then the canvas was overlapped and tied down in place with ropes. Weight had to be distributed evenly on the sled, as excessive weight in the rear would cause the back runners to dig into the snow and make it difficult for the dogs to pull.

The grub box was a wooden affair with a lid, which fit snugly within the bottom of the sled at the rear. In this box were the Primus stove, sugar, tea, hard tack, biscuits, sweetened condensed milk, eating utensils, skillets, hunting knife, salt and pepper, the flour sacks of frozen stews, cocoa, and a small pan for melting snow or ice for drinking water.

With the sled all packed and the frozen seals for dog food and a kerosene lamp lashed down to the very front, it was time to place all the dogs in their respective harnesses. They were stationed two by two with Sally out in front by herself as she was the leader. One always placed two males side by side, never two females since they were prone to fight. The dogs would all be barking and straining at their chains, eager to be on the trail. Julia helped me hitch up the dogs, with Sally the last one to be placed in a harness.

When all was ready and the good-byes had been said, I gripped the handles on the back of the sled and turned the team loose. I hung on for dear life for the dogs were wild and all were running as fast as they could. This they would do for about one-quarter to one-half mile and then settle down to a dog trot. Out on the frozen Arctic Ocean we would begin our journey down the coast.

Mile after mile we proceeded, the dogs all pulling well. I ran along side the sled and once in a while stood on the runners and held on to the handle bars. Sometimes I jumped up on the sled and straddled the load or sat with both legs on the side like some women ride a horse side-saddle. When the temperatures hovered around 30 to 50 below zero you didn't stay on the sled for long. One had to run to keep warm and especially keeping the feet warm.

At noon time the team was halted and I uncapped a thermos of hot cocoa and ate a sandwich. All the dogs laid down. When traveling or working the dogs, I fed then at noon time and again at the end of the day. That day I chopped off hunks of seal and gave each dog a piece about the size of my fist. I kept a close watch on each dog in case one tried to get the other's meat.

An hour later we were on our way. The dogs were going at a steady pace, about as fast as a person can jog. As we approached the end of the day, the dogs slowed down to a walk. We stopped for the night before it got dark. I unharnessed the dogs and tied them up with chains with enough separation so that they couldn't get at each other. I fed them a little larger hunk of seal than they had at noon and they ate snow for moisture. Then they settled down for the night.

With the dogs taken care of, I got out the saw and knife and picked out a drift of solid snow where I lay out a rectangular area which would be my overnight snotell. I cut out blocks of snow approximately 3 x 2 feet and stacked them on top of each other, making four rectangular walls. Across the top I cut blocks longer than 3 feet and leaned them against each other forming the roof. All cracks were filled with loose snow and a small square entrance was made in one end. I unpacked the grub box, sleeping bags, etc. I fired up the Primus stove and, in a skillet, I placed a few frozen pieces of stew. Once they melted and heated up, I had my evening meal. Before turning off the stove, I melted snow for hot water and made my cocoa for the thermoses in the morning and the next day. My kerosene lantern provided light.

I stepped outside before turning in and checked the dogs. I then removed my boots and parka and crawled into my sleeping bag for a good night's sleep. Even though my bed was on frozen ice or snow, I was very comfortable and warm all night.

On these trips I was always impressed by the vast silence that surrounded me. In the village, dogs were barking and children were playing kick ball, but on the trail there was no sound, only your own breathing.

My calculations suggested that I had covered at least 30-35 miles that first day.

The next morning it was difficult to leave my warm cocoon and light the Primus with the temperature in my snow shelter hovering around 35 degrees below zero. I dressed, drank my cocoa, ate a biscuit, which I had thawed out during the night in my sleeping bag. I pulled on my boots and donned my parka, knocked out the walls of my shelter. A second hand snow shelter was seldom used by other travelers, thus we usually pushed out the walls. I then went out to check on the dogs, load the equipment into the sled and prepare for departure. I fed the dogs a small chunk of seal meat and, while they ate, I packed the sled. I lashed everything down so that, should the sled turn over, all the contents wouldn't be lost; you could just stop the team and up-right the sled.

We repeated the previous day's activities, stopping at noon time and camping again that evening. Early in the afternoon we met a team coming from the opposite direction bound for Barrow from Wainwright. It was Ned Nusunginya, the mail carrier, with first class mail for Barrow. He had a team of fourteen dogs; his sled was much larger than mine and heavily weighed down with mail. We stopped our teams[22] and I gave Ned one of my Hershey chocolate bars. We talked of news from Barrow because Ned had been absent for about 3 or 4 weeks on his mail run. We bid each other good-bye and started up our teams.

On the third day I arrived at Wainwright and rolled up to Jim Allen's trading post and home where I remained. His Eskimo helpers unharnessed my dogs, tied them up and fed them. I was made welcome by Jim Allen and his wife Eleanor, while his daughters Kate and Jenny pumped me for hours of Barrow news. I had a letter for Jim Allen from my father and that evening I enjoyed a real home-cooked meal. The Allen girls had a large wind-up console phonograph and we played all the latest records that they secured from the ships the previous summer. Over and over again I played one entitled "Barnacle Bill the Sailor." At bed time I slept on top of my reindeer sleeping bag, as

I was in a heated home, and Mrs. Allen provided me with a blanket and a real pillow.

There were only three white families in Wainwright and I spent 3 days visiting. Rodney Hall, the adopted son of Dick Hall—another trader in the village, was the only white boy there. He had a bicycle, the first I had ever seen, and real soda pop in various flavors. This was a real treat. I called on Mr. and Mrs. Evans, schoolteachers, giving them a letter from my father.

I had a good time and the dogs were rested up. Jim Allen gave me enough seal meat for my trip home and Mrs. Allen made cinnamon rolls for me to take. On the fourth day I began my homeward journey.

*Jim Allen was a friendly member of the Arctic white community who was born in San Francisco's mission district in 1875. Shipwrecked from the* Jesse H. Freeman, *he was befriended by Charles Brower and settled in Wainwright to run a trading post with his native wife, Ellnou* [23]*, who he married in 1903. His life is well-detailed in his autobiography,* A Whaler and Trader in the Arctic, 1895 to 1944.

## MUSHING DOGS

I was the only person in Barrow with a doghouse with twelve stalls. This structure was some 40 feet long and was a lean-to shed attached to the mission oil house. There were stalls on each side about a foot above the ground and a big hook in the rear wall. I put empty gunnysacks, two or three of them, in each stall and they curled up on those. I would put my dogs in there with enough chain to so that they could go to the bathroom in the passageway between them but not fight each other. That's where I kept my dogs at night.

One night, one of my dogs named Sonny[24] got loose, got into a fight with one of my other dogs and was killed. That's what would happen if you didn't get them chained up well. I think I had a better team because I protected them from the elements by putting them in there. Most dogs lived outside and just curled up on the ground, on the snow, and tucked their feet and nose under their bodies.

Unlike the Greenland Eskimo who harness their dogs in a fan shape, the natives of Alaska have their dogs hitched up two by two with a single dog as a leader in front. Each dog has his own harness fitted to him, which is home made from canvas. A good musher always carried two or three spares in the sled.

My team consisted of nine dogs which was a normal team. The rule of thumb was that a dog could pull about 100 pounds.

In a dog team, the leader was usually a female, perhaps because they are smarter. Female dogs have the advantage that they void their bladders completely when they urinate. Males dogs want to stop often and mark multiple spots. When meeting another team the female leader would steer clear of the oncoming team. The leader understands simple commands: "Gee" to the right, "Haw" to the left. I have seen some natives use the command "come gee" and the leader will make a 180 turn to the right and bring the team straight back.

Males are tied to the sled side by side or you can have a female next to a male, but never two females side by side. I don't know why but they always fight. A team can travel 50 miles in one day. They are fed three times a day when they are working, once a day when tied up at home. A normal meal on the trail consisted of a softball-size chunk of seal, walrus or whale meat.

Native dogs can sleep on the snow at -50 to -60 degrees.[25] They curl up and tuck their feet and nose into their underside. When on the trail, dogs will fall asleep after their final feeding and sleep for 8 to 10 hours. Snow can bury them over night. After a storm you can go out to find the dogs and see only white mounds where the dogs are curled up.

## MY FIRST SKIJORING EXPERIMENT

In 1920 my father brought to Alaska a pair of skis. Evidently someone must have suggested that he could do skiing in the Arctic, but as there are no mountains or hills in Barrow, the skis were stored in the warehouse and never used.

One day I had an idea—why couldn't you have dogs pull you on skis? I used only three dogs, two side by side and Sally as the leader. Well, when I got on skis and turned the dogs loose, we went flying across the frozen lagoon. All went well for 200 yards then the team made a right turn—why I don't know—and I went straight ahead. I had to let go of the lead line. The dogs ran back to the house and I had to ski back. I put the skis away and that was the last time I tried that idea. Terza and Julia had been watching me and a good laugh.

## EARLY SCHOOLING

*The government school in Barrow was not always remembered so positively by David's peers. Many found the strict repression of the Iñupiaq language to be intrusive and severe. So strongly did the teachers want the children to learn English that punishment for infractions of the rule was stern and swift. David's parents also did not always agree with the strictness of the punishment. In the August 1932 issue of* The Northern Cross, Dr. *Greist related a story about the expulsion of the church organist, "an eighth grade pupil and a bright one." The fact that such a harsh punishment was handed down by the school after he was found speaking Iñupiaq on school grounds was thought, by Dr. Greist, to be "a little drastic."* (Greist 8/1932:24)

In the government school there was no need for discipline, the Eskimo children were eager to learn and applied themselves diligently to the three "R's." They all learned English quickly and treated this ability as a game.

Barrow school occupied two large rooms when I was a boy. Most of the desks were for two students each. The grades were divided but housed in one room so that the teacher could work with one grade and then move on to another. Later, Mr. Trindle[26] seated five or six students who had finished the eighth grade in an upstairs room where he gave them advanced books to read. They were left alone to study. I, however, never made it that far. I was in the Barrow school for only a short time. I created such a disturbance and, I guess, being white I thought I could get away with it so my folks took me out of the school. Dad ordered a correspondence course from the Calvert System in Baltimore, Maryland which prepared me for high school. The Calvert System was a correspondence course for diplomats and missionaries. Through that I learned English, art, ancient history, and so forth. It was a full course. Dad would lay out the work for me every day and he would help me with it to make sure I was doing it. It was very difficult for me because I wanted to go hunting or running dogs or play kick ball.

*On August 28, 1932 at the age of fourteen, David traveled outside to school. According to* The Northern Cross *of November 1932, he was scheduled to attend high school in California. He sailed on the Patterson and arrived in San Francisco where his mother's brother, Jim Ward, transported him to his half-brother, Elwood Greist, in Santa Paula. He lived with Elwood during that year of school. His parents missed him desperately, lamenting "but every missionary has the same cross sooner or later, if children have been blessed in their home. These boys and girls must be educated, must have benefit of socialized contact if they would be developed for future responsibility." (Greist 11/1932:37)*

In Santa Paula I lived with Elwood and attended a big high school. I took Latin, English and so forth, but I didn't do too well. The only thing I really learned there was typing which I have kept all these years. I got so home sick that year, that when I went back to Barrow, I got to stay.

*Although his parents hoped for his adjustment, David was very home sick during that year. Reportedly he wrote to his friends, explaining "I am coming back to Alaska, all right. I don't seem to fit with these white folks; I am an Eskimo, and Point Barrow is where I belong."* (Greist 3/ 1933:11)

*And return he did. Although they complained about not hearing from him in quite some time, David surprised his parents by returning to Barrow in late 1933 on the* Patterson, *hired on as an assistant to the captain. So miserably was he missed that first year that his parents kept him home the following year. The mission's budget had been cut and it was determined that, at 15 years of age, a year without schooling would "accomplish no irreparable harm."* (Greist 11/ 1933:34)

*After that year at home, however, Dr. Greist seemed to think it was due time for David to return to his schooling. It must have been difficult under the circumstances of a missionary's existence, to raise a child in the ways preferred or thought proper by mainstream culture. Although they had given David much discipline and education at home, they surely felt the need to ensure that their boy approaching manhood would fit into the culture to which he would return. In fact, Dr. Greist wrote to his brother-in-law, Jim Ward in November of 1933, "David now needs regularity, military discipline, and [to] rub up against boys from cultured families, boys of good blood. He has spent so much of his life with the 'raw', and needs nothing further along that line. It is smoothing up he now requires. In such a school as that the boys submit to the management rather than wish to get out every other night to a movie, or other night life. They are chaperoned when out. He needs contact with men of the best traditions of American life and he should get it in the east."*

After that year in California, Dad decided it would be best to send me to a boarding school and he got to corresponding with Mount Vernon School in Vermont and Stony Brook. Mrs. Pederson was in favor of Mount Vernon, but he chose Stony Brook because he got a better scholar-ship for me there. I went out to that one in 1934. On my first trip to school, I took a bus from San Francisco to New York with a stop in Chicago. While there my father's brother, Uncle Lew, met me and, for 2 days, introduced me to the 1934 World's Fair.

### I Go Outside

To those of us in Alaska "to go outside" was to go to the lower 48 states. I was sent to the Stony Brook School for Boys on Long Island, New York the rest of my high school education. I hated to leave my Eskimo friends, my dogs, and my current girl friend, Maria Brower. My parents had other ideas so off I went, leaving Barrow on the MS Patterson in August. Barrow did not have a high school. The eighth grade was the highest attainable grade in the Barrow public school.

In San Francisco my uncle, Jim Ward and his three daughters Maxine, Dorothy—who were in their twenties—and Patsy—who was about my age—met the ship and took me to their home. Aunt Bea, Maxine and Dorothy put American shoes on my feet, bought me a suit, white shirt and replaced my red bandanna handkerchief with a white one. They even re-introduced me to a shower and how to use it. They introduced me to a barber shop where my long hair was cut off. In restaurants I did not know what to order, my first meal was a hot roast beef sandwich; I liked it. A few days later I was put on a Greyhound bus for New York. On my journey from Frisco to New York all I ate were hot roast beef sandwiches with mashed potatoes. I was afraid to try something else.

I arrived in New York and the most frightening feel-ing was being confronted by all of the traffic noise, millions of people, tall buildings, walking on concrete (no tun-dra!) and the heat. At the bus station, I was informed that I had to go from Grand Central Station to the Long Is-land Railroad station in order to take a train to Stony

Brook. I hoisted my duffel bag on my shoulder and started walking. I did not know anything about taxis. I kept asking uniformed policemen for directions. I was wearing my fur parka when I walked down Fifth Avenue and that is when a *New York Times* photographer spotted me, took my picture and asked me a lot of questions. He took me the rest of the way to the train station in his car, showed me how to buy a ticket and what gate to go to for the train. He was very helpful. The caption in *The New York Times* read, "The Costume Which Startled 5th Avenue." To arrive in a city as large as New York from a small village of only 400 people was quite a shock.

I have been told that the Long Island Railroad was the slowest train in the world. Well, I didn't know much about trains, but after several hours the conductor called out Stony Brook! I was then at the boarding school, which would be my home for the next four years. The head master met me at the station and took me to the school. He was Dr. Frank E. Gaebelien, a wise and perceptive man, who saw instantly that I was indeed a stranger in a strange land and a very homesick one at that!

One summer I stayed at Stony Brook and other summers I'd hitchhike to San Francisco and get on the *Patterson* and go to Barrow. This gave me about two or three weeks with my parents and then back to New York. Three summers I did that from 1934 to 1936. I was 20 when I graduated from high school in 1938. I then attended Hanover College in southern Indiana, my father's alma Mater, until World Ward II, at which time I joined the Army Air Corps.

# CHAPTER FIVE
# AROUND THE VILLAGE

*Life in Barrow during the 1920s and 1930s was not unlike life in other small, rural towns. With a very small population and few amenities, social life was simpler and quieter than in other places and times. Entertainment in Barrow was found among friends and family. Spending time together at home, at parties, while playing games, or performing tasks allowed time to develop friendships and provided a pleasurable way of passing the time.*

*The village young people would get together at the hospital, manse, or teacher's quarters for entertainment. They would play games, checkers and Parcheesi. They had a stereopticon with slides from around the world and, later in the Greists' stay, could witness spectacular views coming from the mission movie projector and the handful of "certain old films of clean character" ordered or sent them by supporters.*(Greist 3/1933) *Against the Doctor's wishes they would play cards if they had the chance, even at the hospital after finding cards belonging to Mrs. Greist, an avid bridge player. Such play was put to an end, however, whenever Dr. Greist discovered it. He believed that card playing was incompatible with a good Christian upbringing.*

*As with their peers elsewhere, the teenagers in Barrow liked to congregate and visit. They would have parties on celebratory occasions and holidays with Greist-imposed rules relating one's behavior to one's ability to attend. The Greists had a crank Victrola in the manse and the young people*

61

*would gather to play any record they could collect through the mail or off the summer ships, frequently playing them until they lost their grooves. Those with musical talent— David played the harmonica and banjo—would play for others' amusement and, at one time, several boys even attempted to put together an orchestra.*

*When weather permitted, summer or winter, children of all ages played outdoors. They frequently organized and played a soccer-like game, but enjoyment could also be had taking walks on the tundra and beach, going for picnics, or taking small trips to hunt or seek adventure.*

*Adults also found ways to entertain themselves while interacting with one another. They too enjoyed the films and game playing. Mrs. Greist was an avid reader and the Greists had a significant library. They wrote letters and visited with one another often. Men such as Stanley Morgan were often busy as village handymen to the white population where mechanical contraptions were concerned.[27]*

### ARCTIC RECREATION

I have often been asked when lecturing on life in the Arctic, "What did you do for recreation?" At that time there were no radios or televisions in Barrow and Barrow had no movie theater, nor does it now. At the hospital every Tuesday night the young people would play card games or Parcheesi in the kitchen. I think after a while the school teachers had a certain night of every week for parties at the school for playing games and listening to the phonograph. We would order records COD from Sears and Montgomery Ward catalogs and play them until they wore out. They would be delivered each summer when the parcel packages arrived and consisted mostly of cowboy songs.[28]

In 1933, Dad got a Victor Anamatograph moving picture projector. He ordered alot of comedy films and he used to show them to the kids over and over and they never got tired of them. The Eskimo enjoyed a monkey

*Barrow young people have a Halloween party at the manse, 1931.*

film more than anything else. He had a monkey film that he got from Hollywood and they got the biggest kick out of that. It was about a chimpanzee that had been trained to do different things and they loved that. They called it *The Monkey Film.*

We took the projector out with us in 1936. He used it here in the States to show his film on his lecture circuit to all the different churches and just about wore it out.

Outdoors we often played Anty I Over, a game which may have been unique to Barrow. Half of the group would be on one side of the school building and the other half on the other side. A ball would be thrown from one side to the other over the roof. If a member of the group caught it (it was the honor system) the team would divide and come around the building from both ends. We never knew who had the ball until you were tagged. Some of us would run one way and some the other to the opposite side of the building. Those of us who were tagged were out of the game. Just before you threw the ball over the roof you called out "Anty I Over!"

We also made our own ice skates out of a short piece of 2 x 4 which we would fasten to our boots with seal skin thongs. In a center groove on the underside, we would put blades made from the one and a half inch wide sled runners that Mr. Brower kept in stock at the trading post. The skating season was short, for as soon as the snow covered the lake you could no longer skate.

Girls also had their own games, including *aatchakisaaq.* They would lay a 12 foot 2 x 12 inch plank, called an *aatchakisaun,* across a lump of snow. The toy was very similar to a teeter-totter except that you would stand on one end while another person jumped on her elevated end. You would go high into the air and when you came down, your weight would throw the other person up. Many of the girls became very proficient at this. I saw Julia, Kate, Terza and Maria go up at least 10 to 12 feet and come straight down on the end of the plank. Once you fell off or missed your end of the plank you would let someone else have a turn.

On one occasion, Maria Brower broke her ankle playing this game. Dad advised Mr. Brower to take her outside for proper treatment because he did not have a x-ray machine, etc. Mr. Brower, Maria, and I traveled together to San Francisco on the *Patterson.* I was on my way to school.

Eskimo dances were held in a large building where most of the people could congregate, usually the schoolhouse when I was a boy. The drummers were old men who sat on the floor holding their drums, their legs stretched out in front of them. The oval shaped drums were hand-held— similar to a ping pong paddle. The drums were about 2 feet in diameter, the framework of which was thin wood, and over the frame a thin membrane of walrus intestine was stretched tight. In his other hand each drummer held a flexible wood stick with which he struck the outside frame. Accompanied by singing and chanting the dancers would weave and move in rhythm to the drums. Dancers danced by without partners with stomping feet, the men's motions being more pronounced and vigorous than the women's. You got up on the floor and danced whenever the spirit moved you. Each song or dance lasted 1 to 2 minutes. Dancing was a seasonal form of entertainment, dances being held maybe once a month and rarely during trapping season when most of the men were away from the village.

I think the most popular game was a form of kick ball very similar to soccer; we played that game everyday. Before we had regular soccer balls, we played with a sealskin ball, stuffed with reindeer hair and smaller than a soccer ball—approximately 6 to 8 inches in diameter—and called an *aqsraaq*. The goal posts for the game were usually 100 yards apart and the rules were simple—you could not carry the ball, only kicking was allowed. Frequently, the teams were made up of single men and women against married couples. As the game progressed more and more people would wander in from various parts of the village and participate. During one game there were so many players we had to move the goals about a half-mile apart. Twenty minutes or so could pass before you got to kick the ball.

Sometimes the balls would take a good deal of abuse and a seam would split. In this case, the game would have a time out and one of the girls would sew it back together.

This form of kick ball was only played in the winter, when the ground was frozen and these games often went on until 2:00 or 3:00 in the morning. No artificial lights were used as the moon, stars and northern lights reflected on the white snow and gave us sufficient light to see the ball.

### Burials in the Village

*Prior to the arrival of white missionaries and Christianity, such social institutions as burial were treated very differently than the whites chose to treat them. Subterranean burial was unheard of, in favor of leaving the dead on the tundra surface. Upon their arrival, missionaries established traditional western cemeteries and instructed their converts in the ways of church-based funerals in the name of God and perceived sanitation.*

Prior to Dad and Mother coming to Barrow the natives used to place their dead on top of the ground inland from Barrow. Some in wooden boxes and some without, wild animals or dogs would eventually destroy the bodies and scatter the bones. Behind the village, we found hundreds of human skulls and bones, many weather beaten coffins in various stages of destruction. On a hike inland one summer day we gathered over two hundred skulls and placed them in a pile. I took pictures of them.

Dad gathered the elders of the village together and instructed them on the proper Christian method of burial. During the winter, the dead would be kept in an unheated vacant room in back of the church, where the bodies would be preserved in below zero temperatures. In the summer the mission meat cellar served as the morgue. In the spring the men of the village would dig graves 4 or 5 feet deep into the frozen ground, a task which often took several weeks. Although we never dug one up, I would presume that all of the deceased who were buried in this permafrost were well-preserved.

Mr. Brower furnished the canvas to cover the caskets and he may have even supplied the lumber. He didn't charge them for it. They'd cover the caskets and they'd look real nice. Then on the top of each one someone would draw a cross in pencil or pen. My mother would dress the bodies in clean clothes from the mission boxes.

Dad trained the natives to make the trip to the cemetery in this manner. The sled with the coffin led the procession pulled by four to six young men. Then the widow would follow on a sled. Behind her would be the minister and interpreter followed by all the elders of the church walking two by two. Last would be all of the friends and the congregation following in broken rank. This method was liked very much and it was faithfully carried out during all those years. One year we had seventeen bodies to inter, a result of the flu epidemic, so we used the large 16 foot sled pulled by our tractor with the pump organ and choir on board.

There is one amusing incident that took place concerning burials. The church congregation of 300 was all present at the cemetery behind Barrow during the burial of an old Eskimo man. The men who pulled the sled to the cemetery with the coffin aboard had forgotten the shovels which were needed to cover the coffin after it was lowered into the ground. We all quietly waited while they went back to the church for the shovels. During the quiet wait in the cold, the widow of the elderly citizen sat down on her husband's coffin and lit her pipe for a smoke.

We boys used to target shoot with our bows using tin cans and on some occasions, the human skulls found scattered over the tundra from old burials.

On one particular day I shot an arrow at a skull and hit it. A bird flew out. I ran over and picked up my arrow and the skull. Inside was a bird nest with six eggs. I carried it back to the village and my mother blew the eggs, wrapped the eggs in cotton and, with the skull, shipped it to the Children's Museum in Indianapolis. It can still be seen today at that museum, but I don't think they know that I was responsible for it being there.

### Every Sunday

*Every Sunday, Dr. Greist was responsible for performing three sermons. Early Sunday morning services would be held at the Utqeagvik Presbyterian Church in Barrow and immediately following, he would travel 6 miles to Point Barrow to perform a service there. Upon his return he might attend to various activities and rest until a third service at the Barrow church. While this was going on, David's mother was often nursing at the hospital, allowing everyone else to participate in church services. Sunday school was also taught during the day. David was left to his own devices, attending church and doing the required chores before having time to himself.*

We had two great big pot-bellied stoves in the church that we fired up. One of the elders or the janitor from the hospital or, sometimes, I would go over and do that. My father let the natives run their own evening services on Sunday in their own language and everything. One of the elders would take over and they enjoyed that, enjoyed doing it themselves.

On Sunday morning Dad used an interpreter. During the church service, Dad would say a few sentences then stop and either Lee Suvlu or Roy Ahmaogak would interpret and then he'd say a few more words and so forth. The church services were attended by everyone in the village. Mr. Brower didn't attend and Mr. Hopson didn't go. I don't think Mr. Brower ever came to church, but his family did.

He would use interpreters for baptisms, too. Sometimes he would baptize eight or nine babies at the same time. One time he married five couples at the same time. A picture of that was in *Time* magazine years ago. Those couples traveled all the way down from the east to get married. Dad had to use an interpreter for that wedding because some of them didn't understand English.

During one early church service some young men brought a partially paralyzed grandmother into the church and placed her on a deer skin on the floor near the big coal burning stove. Alongside her they placed a chamber pot that a former missionary had given her. The ushers carried out this vessel when necessary and then returned it to her side. They were all accustomed to this and all was done without any concern to anyone. Only the whites in the congregation held their breath, closed their eyes and accepted the custom. She was a confirmed Christian and the only effort she made was to go to church every Sunday. This continued, when she was able, until she died an old woman while we were there.

One day a member of the parish, an old Eskimo woman in her 90s with a complete set of teeth, came to see Dr. Greist at the hospital. She was frail and was brought in on a sled. Her mind was alert and she asked Dr. Greist to pull two of her teeth. Dad examined her mouth and asked through Helen, "Which one aches?"

Helen said, "She says they do not hurt."

"Why does she want them pulled?"

She says, "That other people in the village got teeth pulled and she wants them like that too."

Dr. Greist said, "Helen tell her that she is a very fortunate person and she should thank God she has such good teeth. I will not pull them unless she needs it done."

## ARCTIC NEWS: *THE NORTHERN CROSS*

The Northern Cross *newsletter was published by the Greists from 1928 to 1936. It became an excellent means of not only broadcasting the successes and range of activities at the Barrow mission, but also of documenting daily life as the missionaries and their charges experienced it. It described the tiny Presbyterian enclave of the North and allowed those in far away places a glimpse of the exotic.*

*A better serial with a unique cast of characters and plots could not have been had for the price. Those who contributed to the mission received copies, as did others who sent their $1 per year subscription for the, sometimes, quarterly publication. It would take days to produce the newsletter and a regular mailing of the publication contained between 550 and 750 pieces. Through the* Cross *the Greists documented their last years in Barrow with vivid detail and an air of promotion of the village and people who they, at once, loved and held familiar, yet continued to find unpredictable and marvelous.*

Dad would type up the stencils on his typewriter and he would have one of the Eskimo young people who was a good artist draw the cover sheet.[29] Then he would show

*My mother, Miss Komedal, I, and Julia preparing the Northern Cross for mailing.*

them how to do it on the stencil and then we would run them off on the mimeograph. Then all the kids from the hospital—workers and ambulatory patients—would come over to the manse and we would put them all together, staple them together, put the covers on, paste them into containers, and put the addresses on them. We'd spend several days and nights doing that and then we'd take them over to Mr. Brower and he'd have to cancel all the stamps, of course, and ship them on Ned's sled down the coast. They were bulky, but they didn't weigh very much. There were an awful lot of them. Dad should have charged more than $1, but in those days a dollar was a lot of money.

He started writing them in Nenana and continued in Barrow. Whenever he could, he'd go ahead and write it up. I think it was just to let the people in the States know what was going on and inform them the activities of the mission, especially those churches that were donating so much to help out. This was a way of thanking them and letting them know what their contributions were doing for the people. Some of the issues had some interesting stories in them. Dad was quite a storyteller and I think he had a pretty good sense of humor.

### A Lasting Image

*Not only did the Greists use words to document their time in Barrow, but also pictures. During his time in the Arctic, Dr. Greist took pictures, moving and still which created a legacy used still by researchers to interpret arctic history and culture. Portraits, landscapes, and processual photographs and movies captured the ways people spent their time and the difficult circumstances with which they had to contend.*

*Additionally the images captured the boyhood of their son growing up on the North Slope. From a toddler being cared for by Iñupiat baby-sitters to a fine young man driving his own dogteam and sailing the high seas, the chronicle is telling of a missionary's child.*

Dad must have gotten his Devry movie camera in 1930; he must have ordered it. My half-brother in California recommended a certain make for him and Dad sent him a check for it. He sent it up to him and, when the Lindberghs were there, the Colonel gave him instructions on how to use it. The old Devry movie camera was a 35 mm. Film went through there pretty fast.

To print photographs, all the whites would get together, save up all our films and then go down to the schoolhouse. They would darken the room and hang blankets around. You had all your developer in there and you would put your developing paper behind your negatives, take it out into the light for a few seconds and take it back in and develop it. You'd make up your own hypo and fixer and count "thousand one, thousand two, thousand three..." If you held it too long, you'd have a dark picture.

The negatives came in rolls on a wooden spool with paper on one side and film on the other and when you'd take them into the darkroom, you'd peel the paper off and dip it in the developer until you began to see your image.

## A WHALE OF A TALE

*The Iñupiat culture is closely identified with the bowhead whale and the process of whaling. Although the whales contribute significantly to the nutritional well-being of Iñupiat households, they also contribute to the emotional well-being of the Iñupiat culture. In the Arctic, the spiritual connection between whale and whaler is expressed through the tradition that surrounds whaling and the importance placed upon that tradition. Prescriptions for everything from clothing to conduct place whaling into a category of things sacred. Such attention to detail has guaranteed the preservation of not only the process, but also, it is believed, man's ability to continue whaling through the appeasement of the animal and its spirit.*

*Commercial whalers succeeded in sailing to the Arctic by the mid 1800s and established constant and profitable contact with the Iñupiat people which changed the culture forever. A trade system of western goods, established years earlier through contact with villages along Alaska's western coast, was enhanced. Western goods became more plentiful and available than ever and their perceived need grew with the economy. The whale oil market thrived for the next 50 years and was later enhanced by the baleen market driven by a European hunger for buggy whips, corsets, and parasol. Baleen remained profitable until the early 20th century when changing fashion and the invention of celluloid left no reason for the whaling industry to remain in the Arctic. Although a few whalers stayed behind as traders, most left the arctic waters and the whales to the Iñupiat.*

*In the spring, whaling takes place around April and May when leads—channels of open water between the large sheets of floating ice—begin to form in the ice miles off the coast. After a month or more of preparation, whaling crews take their place on the ice along the water's edge and patiently await the bowhead whales making their annual migration eastward.*

*The following fall, whaling takes place around September and October as the water opens, the Arctic Ocean is free of land-locked ice and the bowhead population begins its southwestward migration. The whaling crews can remain land-based as they watch for signs of passing whales, launch from the shore, and intercept the whales. In either season, successful whaling requires patience, quiet, luck, and skill.*

*At either season, a flurry of activity begins on shore once a whale is killed. In the past, a watch person would watch the seas and alert the village when a successful crew's flag was flown, indicating the capture of a whale. Today, a CB radio call to shore notifies all of the good news and a flood of snowmachines carrying extra hands to help in butchering the whale ensues.*

The whale, the greatest and largest mammal on earth, is very important to the Eskimo. During my time in Barrow, its meat fed over seven hundred dogs. The blubber was used to heat the stoves.[30] The leather-like skin and blubber or *maktak* was eaten raw or cooked. The skin is a soft, black substance about one to one and a half inches thick and is fastened to the blubber underneath. *Maktak* is easily cut with a steak knife into small pieces which you pop into your mouth and chew. The small amount of blubber with it helps it to go down. It has a terrible taste and I do not recommend it to the novice. As a lad growing up in Barrow I acquired a taste for it.

I am personally acquainted with the bowhead whale[31], which is numerous in the Arctic Ocean. Whalebone or baleen is found in the mouth of the bowhead instead of ivory teeth. Baleen is black and lines the jaws like leaves of a book. Fine hairs on the inside edges help to strain out plankton and other crustaceans which are held back and swallowed through a small throat when the whale opens its mouth and takes in water, the water is then expelled through the mouth, not through the top blow hole. Years ago baleen was used for corset stays and buggy whips, very little use is made of whalebone today. I have seen baleen taken from the whale's mouth measuring up to 12 feet, the tongue can weigh as much as 1,800 pounds.

Whales are caught in both spring and fall. A crew of fifteen to thirty men[32] comprise the crew of the *umiak*, a skin boat about 30 feet in length.[33] Back then the village of Barrow normally produced six or seven crews. The *umiak* was lashed to a flat sled pulled by dogs and hauled out onto the ice pack to a lead, open water where the arctic ice pack has separated. Through this lead the whales journeyed north, past Barrow on into the Arctic Ocean and Beaufort Sea. We didn't see them again until fall when they made their return trek south, many with young. The larger mammals weighed between 60 and 70 tons.

The whalers took up the long, lonely vigil at the edge of the ice. Teenagers were seldom permitted at the camps, because conversation was not allowed. The whale has a keen sense of hearing even though the entrance of the ear is about the size of a pencil lead. There was always one man on duty watching the surface of the water for movement. When a whale was spotted blowing and taking in fresh air, the rest were alerted in whispers. The gunner took his place in the bow. His darting gun and shoulder gun loaded and ready, the *umiak* was maneuvered into position where it was hoped the whale would come up for air. When the whale did blow and began to go under, the neck area behind the head was exposed. That was the fatal spot. The gunner fired the shoulder gun which shot a 6 inch projectile into the whale and, a few seconds later, a muffled explosion was heard. In the mean time harpoons were thrust into the body with long lines attached to inflated seal pokes—sealskins that have been cleaned, their openings sealed, and inflated to drag on the surface of the water. Thus the location of the animal could be determined if it sounded during its death throes. Whales have been known to dive straight down for two thousand feet, their bodies adjust to the tremendous pressure. When the whale died it would float to the surface, exposing a small part of its black body resembling the top of a submarine lying low in the water.

When a whale was caught, the crew's flag was run up on a pole on the top of an iceberg. The village was alerted, school was let out, the entire village with dog teams drove out to the camp to help butcher and pull it up onto the ice. Block and tackle were used to fasten to the tail and, with all of the people pulling and chanting, the whale was slowly pulled up onto the ice while men with flensing knives began to cut away the *maktak* and blubber and meat.

A cook tent was set up where gallons of hot tea and homemade doughnuts[34] were available to all. No one stopped working. If the wind changed, bringing in the ice and closing the lead, the whale would be lost. As the whale was cut up, each head of a family would drag a portion of the blubber and meat across the ice to the waiting sleds and transport it to the village and the meat cellars. All piles were as equal in size as could be. The captain of the crew received the tail—supposed to be the best part—and the baleen from the mouth, the only cash item of the whole animal.

*A tail of a whale or a whale of a tale!*

The work went on all night; the sun did not go down during this time so we worked in daylight night and day. After 18 hours all that remained on the ice were the head bone and ribs, these were allowed to go back into the sea. The area was then deserted and the whalers went back to their silent vigil of watching and waiting for the next whale. A good whale season yielded eight whales.

You have heard of the "one that got away?" Well on one such occasion we had "one that got away." During its death throes it sounded, but did not come back up in the open lead. We believed that it came up under the solid ice pack but where, no one could guess. A few days later the dogs began pawing and sniffing in a certain section of the ice pack on which we had our camp. With axes and shovels we began to chop a hole in the ice, after several hours the pressure of gas in the whale's stomach caused it to rise and up popped a 60 foot whale!

### NA - LU - KA - TAQ

*Summer is a time for celebration in the Arctic. Various subsistence activities are in full swing and the all-hours daylight illuminates the open water and the activity that the relatively warm weather fosters. Temperatures can soar into the 50s and the sea opens long enough from July to September to invite boating and late summer walrus and seal hunts.*

*Held to celebrate the previous fall and spring's whaling success, the annual* nalukataq *is a means for the community to share in the good fortune of the crew whose skill and perseverance landed the whale. The festival is a system for redistributing resources, a way for a primary food source to be divided equally among all society's members. Additionally,* nalukataq *is a celebration of the whale from whom both spiritual and nutritional nourishment is derived. It is an expression of honor and thanks for the whale's giving of himself toward the survival of a respectful community.*

*In Barrow today,* nalukataq *is normally held in June on the beach. Canvas and plastic wind breaks have replaced the overturned* umiaks *as shelter. Pilot crackers, Eskimo dough-nuts, and tea are distributed with* maktak, *whale meat, whale flipper, goose soup and* mikigaq —*chunks of whale meat and tongue fermented in blood. The extremely costly affair is al-most always thrown by multiple successful* umialiks *or boat captains whose crews share the intense labor needed to stage such an event. The festivals for individual whales are, thus, consolidated, allowing people to miss a minimum of time from jobs and other obligations placed on their lives by the late 20th century.*

Probably the most known celebration in the Arctic, *nalukataq*[35] was recorded by Arctic whalers in the 1800s. A celebration for a successful whale hunt, the big event would take place in July on the beach at Barrow where skin boats would be turned on their sides to provide shel-ter from the wind. The entire population—men, women, and children, native and white—attended.

For weeks preceding the event the women and girls would busy themselves making new fur or seal skin boots for their husband, brother or boyfriend. Colorful snow shirts were made to cover their fur parkas, the men's shirts being of solid colors and the women's of various designs—the more gaudy the better!

The captain and crew who caught the whale were hosts at the gala affair. Four to seven walrus hides were sewn together to form a round jumping blanket, a *nalukataq,* about 12 feet in diameter with hand holds around the outside. The four corners would be supported by stout ropes anchored to the sand over a cross tee made by two long poles. The jumping skin was then stretched so that it was 4 feet above the sand. Forty to fifty of us would take a handhold with our left hand, facing the fellow's back in front with your right hand on his or her shoulder, all of us facing the same direction. Then some poor victim would get into the middle of the skin to jump. With rhythm, pulling the skin taut and with grunts, groans and chant-ing we would slowly toss the jumper into the air. Some

*Julia being tossed high in the air at* Nalukatag.

would kick their feet and legs to keep upright and just as he or she was about to hit the skin would stiffen legs, lock knees, smack the skin and up again he would go. The better jumpers would go 30 to 50 feet in the air. When you fell over or lost your balance you got off the skin and someone else had a turn.

Terza, Julia, Maria and Kate were all good jumpers. David Brower, sometimes at the top of his jump, would throw out a handful of cigarettes.[36] On one such occasion, everyone let go of the skin and scrambled for the smokes, poor David came down on a loose and spent skin.

One time a fellow was thrown up into the air at an angle and he came down from 40 feet onto the hard sand breaking his leg. We took him to Dad at the hospital in a sled pulled by a bunch of us boys. Julia was top heavy and she had difficulty coming down and hitting the skin with her feet. Terza, when up in the air, would tuck both legs up under her body at an angle and then would straighten them out just before she hit the skin. She was quite graceful.

The jumping went on from early morning to late afternoon. When the adults took a break from *nalukataq* we kids would try our hand at jumping. There were so many of us that we did a pretty good job of tossing our bodies into the air. We had a hard time tossing a heavy person up very high. When everyone was finished the skin would be loosened and placed on the sand in front of the people sitting behind the upturned skin boats. While the jumping on the skin was going on many of the old men would whittle and make arrows for us boys. We all looked forward to that.

Eight to ten old men would start up a chanting song and beat a rhythm on their homemade drums. Then the dancing would begin—no touching or holding, everyone dancing individually. The women would bounce up and down and move their arms and hands through the air very much like swimming under the water. The men would stomp their feet, first one then the other. Their arm and hand motions were abrupt, their heads jerking up and down to the rhythm of the drums.

A break in the dancing would occur while a feast of hard tack, tea, *maktak,* and meat was consumed by all. The owner of the boat catching the whale would bring the tail of the whale, which was supposed to be the best part, up from his meat cellar. This would be cut up and passed around to all.

After the feast the dancing would begin again until two or three in the morning with the sun still shining low on the horizon.

*Although Dr. Greist, as resident missionary, "never condemned it, per se," he did view Iñupiat dancing as a suspect activity due to its continuance long into the night and its participants' "resulting incapacity for the hunt." (Greist 1/1931:7) David, on the other hand, embraced the dance as he did other portions of Iñupiat culture. Beginning at a young age, he danced at many a* nalukataq, *as did his mother.[37]*

*Young David at an Iñupiat dance.*

## Dad's Walrus Hunt

The only walrus hunt I was ever involved in was from the MS Patterson. We were cruising through and around ice near Wainwright in July of 1932 when we spotted several bulls sunning themselves on an ice field. We lowered a boat and Captain Pederson's son was selected to shoot one. The boat approached the ice floe and the bulls did not even try to leave the ice. We pulled it aboard with block and tackle.

My father had a very different experience while living at Cape Prince of Wales. There he noticed that the village sled dogs were ill-fed, poor and relatively few in number. Meat cellars were empty and although the village was hungry for meat, reindeer were largely neglected or were strayed, scattered or lost. He was left to ponder why, with so many whales passing within sight and the innumerable walrus heard off shore as they sunned themselves on the ice floes, was this scarcity of dog feed?

Eighteen months earlier, 192 or more adults had died from the "flu." Nearly every expert whaler, bear hunter and leader of the semi-annual walrus hunt had died; men recognized as the hunters of the village. The younger men had never assumed the responsibility in these matters, having been merely helpers, regarded as novices or beginners. Therefore, for want of courageous leadership, the young men remained closely within the village caring for nearly two hundred orphans left as a result of the sickness.

The young men stood about the beach in groups, listening to the booming howl of walrus as they passed going north into the Arctic. Day after day they hesitated to launch their great *umiaks.*

Henry, a middle aged Eskimo who had strangely escaped death during the epidemic, was persuaded by my father to get together a crew of ten for a walrus hunt. My father, an expert with rifle and pistol, would accompany them. When all was ready they were able to launch two *umiaks* with twenty men. Dad went in the first boat with Henry. He had prepared his own food for he could not stomach pickled seal meat, seal oil or sourdough doughnuts fried in seal oil.

A cask of fresh water, many rifles, hunting knives, sails, oars and paddles were stowed in the boat. A small Primus oil stove was also carried for when the crew would go upon an ice pan to prepare meals.

I will now narrate the story as told me by my father.

"We sailed in the late afternoon and at 4 a.m. the following morning we heard walrus barking as distant thunder. We were eating breakfast on an ice pan many acres in size. Tea had been brewed for all when a startling booming sound was heard, at which all the Eskimo sat rigidly erect. A great crack had formed breaking our ice pan in two and separating us from our boat. The crack rapidly widened and men had to run and jump across to get to the boat. They launched the boat and paddled to our portion of the ice pan, hauled up the boat alongside our group at tea. We were again startled by the distant howling of walrus. A young man climbed the mast and, with my binoculars, studied the distant ice.

"Quickly stowing the tent, food stuffs and water we rushed to the boat and carried it to the water, launched it, silently and with sails set all hands paddling quietly. With no spoken word we headed directly to the immense field where the walrus were said to be. The intervening ocean was as quiet as a mill pond owing to the presence of the ice. After five miles the lookout whispered that the walrus were near.

"Three men with rifles were stationed, alternately, with as many pike men on the port side and starboard side. I was placed at the stern next to Lewis Tungwenok who would interpret orders to me.

"Suddenly we were surrounded by a vast number of female walrus many of whom had calves at their side. They were playing, diving and rolling about in the sea. The calves were having the time of their lives, sometimes riding on the backs of their mothers, struggling to get back on. The females surrounded us closely and fearlessly. There were at least two hundred mothers and many young.

"Suddenly the sail was lowered, and the men ordered to fire. A walrus is difficult to kill. Their thick skin can turn a bullet. A hit in the head with a high powered rifle would do the trick. Otherwise wounded, the animal will dive for the depths and usually an unwounded walrus will follow and hold the injured animal on the bottom until he empties his lungs of air thus escaping the enemy.

"Someone had unwittingly wounded a calf, and its cries, almost human in character, instantly created a startling change. With the wounded calf screaming with pain, apparently every female walrus attacked our light skin boat. Some dived underneath our boat attempting to push their tusks through the boats bottom, and others rushed to the sides and attempted to place their great tusks, 18 to 20 inches in length, over our gunwales and capsize the *umiak*.

"This is when the pike men came into play. A pike is a very short, thick-bladed knife attached to a pole some 10 feet in length. They thrust these pikes deeply in the water along side the boat, the walrus attacking the boat were thus wounded and moved away. The pike men were kept busy with Henry screaming orders in fear that the flimsy boat might be capsized. A person falling into the ice-filled Arctic Ocean will perish in 10 to 15 seconds unless pulled to safety. Fortunately our boat came safely out from the melee.

"All became suddenly quiet as death. Not a walrus remained on the surface. Apparently at some signal given by the walrus themselves, all dove below the surface and remained there. We quickly harpooned the dead animals, twelve in all, each weighing hundreds of pounds. These were drawn up on the ice by block and tackle to be cut up at leisure. The surrounding sea for some acres was as red as though composed of blood.

"We had noted a bull walrus lying upon an ice floe 200 yards away from the water sunning himself, at times raising his head to look about. He seemed unconcerned however with the royal battle nearby. The mother walrus will not tolerate the presence of a male when the calves are young. He was keeping his distance.

"I was permitted to shoot this bull with my Springfield .30-06. Killed readily we hauled him with difficulty by hand over the intervening ice to the water's edge where he was butchered with the females. We now had thirteen large animals and, when cut up, they made a very heavy load, filling our skin boat almost to the gunwales. Our boat rode deep in the water with only 6 inches of gunwale showing.

"With a choppy sea our boat could not have safely held the load, but with a sea full of floating ice, the wind seemingly had little effect. All skins and fleshy parts were loaded, the bony parts of the skeletons were discarded. The long tusks of ivory were saved.

"We sailed for home. All went to sleep except the steersman and this author who was more than anxious concerning the overloaded ship.

"In time, after making rapid progress with a strong wind, we landed. Great was the rejoicing within the village because of the meat brought in not only by us, but the other boat as well. Our load, however, was by far the largest.

"I had enjoyed the unique sport and had the satisfaction of knowing that I had some small share in filling the meat cellars of the village. Subsequently there seemed no further hesitation as to hunting at sea. Frequent trips were made for more walrus and even whales. The dogs grew fat and the puppies were happy.

"I remained ashore busying myself in the work of the missionary physician about the village. This was to be our last summer at Wales."

### Planes in the Arctic

Joe Crosson, one of Alaska's aviation pioneers, came in with one of the first planes. He brought in serum for the diphtheria epidemic of 1930 in an open cockpit plane. That's the first airplane I remember. When airplanes first started coming it didn't really change things very much. Of course we all ran down to see them land because it was so unusual. Once he landed, Crosson would drain the oil out of his engine, take it to the hospital and keep it warm on the register of the furnace until he was ready to go, when he would put the warm oil back into the engine. Planes didn't come very often, only in emergencies, because people didn't have the money to pay for a trip going up like that. I remember one time when Crosson came and was real tired. Mother made him go to sleep in her own bed because she knew he was fatigued.

*The Lindbergh plane on the lagoon at Barrow, Aug. 1931. Lindy showing Stanley Morgan the radio system. Beverly is in the white parka.*

### Mother's Last Plane Ride

*During their service in Alaska, the Greists ventured outside the state only twice. In 1929, the family left following the burning of the manse (see* A Winter's Fire) *and in 1934, when Mrs. Greist traveled outside for medical attention. Jenny Brower, daughter of Charles Brower and a trained nurse, had recently arrived in the village and she agreed to fill the gap left by Mrs. Greist's absence. Dr. Greist's brother, coming for a visit, flew with Mrs. Greist from Fairbanks to Barrow on her return trip.*

*David's Uncle Lew stayed in Barrow until August and returned to the States on the US Revenue Cutter Northland.*

The only close relative to ever visit us at Barrow was my father's brother, Lewis T. Greist, a prominent lawyer in Chicago. He and Dad were of the same stature and close in age.[38] Uncle Lew had always wanted to visit Barrow while we were there. Finally in 1934 he wrote Dad and suggested that now was the time when he could come. My mother happened to be in the States at that time for much needed dental work and other medical problems, but she was ready to return to Barrow. Uncle Lew contacted her and they met in Seattle, took the *Victoria* to Seward and the railroad to Fairbanks with a stop at Curry, where all got off for the night.

Joe Crosson, famous bush pilot of Alaska, offered to fly them to Barrow for $80. He met them at the train and introduced Uncle Lew and Mother to Bobbie Robbins who would take them to Barrow. Joe's wife was expecting a baby and she begged him not to leave on such a hazardous trip at that time. Joe assured Mother of Bobbie Robbins' ability, that he had been a pilot in World War I. His mechanic, who would fly with them, was Fred "Shorty" Williams. The plane was a single engine five passenger Stinson. Uncle Lew and Mother went to the market and picked up 100 pounds of potatoes, 100 pounds of green onions and a crate of eggs (30 dozen). They had to leave Fairbanks as soon as possible while the snow was hard and still on the ground, so the plane could use skis, as skis would have to be used to land at Barrow. Beside a canary in a cage that Mother carried on her lap, there were cameras, film, guns, ammunition, tools, medicine, and food stuffs. Uncle Lew sat by a window on a crate of potatoes, taking movies, Mother sat on a crate of eggs holding onto the canary by the other window. All of the seats had been taken out to make room for cargo.

The next day, April 22nd, they took off for Barrow. All went well until they landed on the Koyukuk River at Bettles, 185 miles north of Fairbanks. This was Jack Dodds' place where they would fill up with gasoline. In landing on the frozen river one of the skis broke and the plane lurched one way and then the other. After bumping along the plane came to rest facing the opposite direction, there were no brakes on skis. Mother screamed and the bird fell on the floor chirping. Uncle Lew was on the floor and all of the baggage, foods and merchandise was in a jumbled pile with Mother on top of it, tears all over her face and hands full of broken eggs. The cabin was a mess. Shorty

Williams helped Mother up saying, "Come on Mrs. Greist, everything is all right. I'll get you out of this mess in a few minutes."

"What happened?" Mother asked, "Why didn't you tell me that you were going to land like that?" "Oh no," said Shorty, "we don't usually land like that. One of the skis broke when we landed and messed things up. We'll fix it."

A dog team drove to the plane from the settlement. "Here is a dog sled to take you both to Jack Dodds' cabin on the shore," said Shorty.

Jack Dodds maintained a home for wayfarers, and travelers. His place was known far and near as the cleanest, the homiest, and the very most welcome of all within the Far North. Jack was a left-over from the gold rush days of 1898. He was small of stature and doubled up from some disease or injury. He lost his fortune during the gold rush days, but decided to remain in Alaska and went into the roadhouse business. My mother said that he served the nicest bread and the very best flapjacks she had ever eaten away from home. She asked Jack, "How do you do it?" He told her, "I got my starter 40 years ago and I kept the jug going by adding sugar, potato water and flour after each rising." The jug was not permitted to freeze and was kept in a warm place. Jack further remarked, "I add a small amount to my batch bread or the makings of flap jacks the night before... does the trick." Jack was one of the old-timers, the men who made Alaska—hardy men, men of brains, blood and brawn. Very few are left.

On Tuesday, April 24th they took off for Barrow. After crossing the Endicott Mountains, the entire tundra and coast were engulfed in fog. Robbins elected to turn back and again landed at Bettles. On April 26th, again they attempted to reach Barrow and on the other side of the Endicotts, found fog again, turned around again and this time went back to Fairbanks in order to take off with skis. Although the snow was melting and getting soft at

Fairbanks, they chose a frozen lake 65 miles southeast of Fairbanks as the departure point. After a night's stay, Mother, Lewis and cargo were taken there by bus. The plane was already there.

On April 27th, another start was made for Barrow. Fog again was encountered and a return was made to the lake. By this time Mother had had her fill of airplanes and asked Robbins if she could wait for the summer ships and go to Barrow on one. His reply, "No sir lady, I started to get you to Barrow for a certain price and that is what I am going to do! I have already lost $2,000 on this deal so far but you, Mrs. Greist are going with me. That is an order."

April 28th was their fourth attempt to reach Barrow. This time another companion plane was on the same lake also going to Barrow. Both planes left together and flew in loose formation, both stopping at Bettles for fuel. After crossing the Endicotts, the sun came out and there was no fog. After five hours Barrow came into view and both planes landed on the frozen lagoon near the hospital. I was able to get a movie of the plane landing. We were never able to get Mother into another plane.

## HARLEY DAVIDSON GOES NORTH

*The Arctic presented constant logistical challenges to missionaries as they tried to spread their word over the great territories to which they had been assigned. Dr. Greist regularly traveled to Wainwright and Point Barrow and found travel with hired dogs uncomfortable and uncertain, slow and harrowing. After pleading with the Board of Missions to supply him with a dogteam and accouterment and after receiving donations from supporters for the purchase of team, sled, corral supplies, and feed, he determined that the upkeep of such a team would be too great and pursued other transportation options.*

*In The Northern Cross he complained that while he had asked the Board of Missions for adequate transportation, he had been flatly refused. The Board of Missions considered*

*such expenditure unwise and the Doctor believed that he and
his parishioners were the victims of anti-arctic prejudice.*

*On advice from Roald Amundson, he decided to try the
motorcycle.*

In 1923 Captain Amundsen, the famous Norwegian
explorer, was a guest in our home in Barrow. Once after
dinner, a lengthy conversation followed concerning transportation in the Arctic. It was discussed whether a faster
method of travel could be developed to replace the dog
team. Amundsen mentioned that in Norway motorcycles
with sidecars and skis were successfully used. He urged
my father to try the motorcycle and, for several years, Dad
did ponder the idea. Six years later in 1929, after confer-
ring with the other white men in Barrow—there were only
five—as to the feasibility of such a contraption, Dad decided to order one from the States.

Captain John Backland, master of the *CS Holmes,* was
contacted in Seattle to purchase and bring to Barrow a
1930 Harley Davidson Big Twin. Captain Backland delivered it to Barrow during the summer of 1930 at a cost of
$800. It was equipped with windshields, leg protectors, a
side car, skis and chains for the back drive wheel. The skis
were made of hickory, four feet long and sheathed on the
bottom with steel. With the machine Dad anticipated a
trip to Wainwright would take one day rather than 3 days
by dog sled.

We put the thing together in the fall with the help of
Stanley Morgan, also a trained mechanic. I was chosen to
be the driver and Sergeant Morgan gave me my first lesson in operating the motorcycle. I was thirteen, already
nearly 6 feet tall and thrilled beyond measure.

The machine worked fine on the frozen lagoon, but
when we encountered soft snow the drive wheel would
sink down and the cycle would stop. I would then get off
and the passenger out of the sidecar and we would lift the
entire machine out of the snow and onto firmer ice. Although it had problems, it was still the fastest thing that

*The Harley Davidson back in the States, sans skiis.*

had ever been in Barrow. I would take kids for rides on the lagoon up to 25 or 30 miles per hour, pulling small sleds.

It proved to be a miserable failure. It could not be reliably used on Dad's missionary trips down the coast. It was finally decided that the dog team was the most reliable and safest mode of travel in the Arctic. So with our team of eight to twelve dogs my father continued his missionary journeys to the outlying settlements until he left Barrow in 1936 to retire in Indiana. The motorcycle was stored in the basement of the hospital never to be used in the Arctic again.

In 1935 when I made my second trip out to Stony Brook School, the Harley went on the ship with me to San Francisco where I assembled it and drove it to New York. I used it all through college, finally selling it just prior to my entering the Air Corps in 1942.

### THE SNOWMOBILE
One year Sergeant Stanley Morgan ordered a Model T Ford from Seattle equipped with a caterpillar tread drive and skis on the front wheels. When the chassis arrived on

the *CS Holmes,* Morgan, James Ford—a visiting archaeologist from New York, and Mr. Trindle, the current school
teacher, built on a cabin complete with bunks and a heat-
ing/cooking stove. Early in April when all was ready they
wheeled the machine out of the warehouse where they
had been working on it and prepared to give it a trial run.
He began his journey through the village between the
homes and had not gone more than 100 yards when he
ran into an iron rod in front of Solomon's house. It was
sticking up through the snow and had once had a dog
tied to it. It pierced the radiator, causing a delay of several
weeks for repairs. By the time the radiator was repaired
the snow was gone. I really don't know if that vehicle ever
did perform efficiently in the winter.

Two years later Morgan again ordered a car. This time
it was a Model A Ford with improved treads, more power
and more speed. A similar cabin was built on the chassis.
After several trial runs Sergeant Morgan and Mr. Trindle
decided to take it on a long trip to the area east from
Barrow where the delta of the Colville River is located.
Behind the snowmobile they pulled a trailer loaded down
with their supplies, gasoline and extra parts in the event of
a break down. All went well until they were crossing
Harrison Bay which, in October, was not sufficiently frozen. The heavy trailer broke through, pulling the
snowmobile down with it. Luckily the water was only 4
feet deep and all the occupants got out safe but soaked to
the skin with ice water. They hurried to a nearby cabin on
the bay shore, dried out and then, with native help, went
back and disconnected the trailer from the snowmobile
and pulled both out. After drying out the distributor and
the plug wires, the engine started right up. This, even with
it having been in salt water for four days. Needless to say,
they did not continue their journey. They made a 180
degree turn and high-tailed back to Barrow.

When my wife Alicia and I visited Barrow in 1971, I
observed a notable absence of dogs. When I lived there

there were 700+ dogs in the village. During our trip we counted five or six. We soon learned that each family had a modern snowmobile, sometimes two. Purchased from Brower's store, the machines had replaced all the sleds and dogs in Barrow. By then oil was being pumped out of Prudhoe Bay and the natives were well-heeled. They could afford luxuries such as VCRs, televisions, radios, electric stoves and snowmobiles. Gone were the dogs and sleds. I don't know what happened to Morgan's Model A. It was gone like the dogs and sleds. Progress!

## A New Sled

*Although the motorcycle proved to be a failure and the 'snowmobile' was a moderate success, the mission was not without reliable transportation. Over the years, sleds were made for Dr. Greist. Driven by Iñupiat members of the church with dogteams, Dr. Greist was able to travel around the North Slope, ministering to his patients and the faithful. As David matured and his dogteam grew, they too proved useful in providing mission transportation.*

There were seven different teams that Dad used and they would use their own sleds. Dad had two different sleds made for himself, one with a seat in it for his use. When we had our own team our sled was used. Then I had a work sled of my own which I used for hauling my whale meat. It was too dirty to be used for anything else. I don't remember who made it for me, but when I left Lee Sulvu took charge of all my dogs and everything.

After Dad had been in Barrow 3 years it was decided that he needed a new sled. Dog sleds were normally 3 feet wide and 12 to 15 feet long with hickory runners[39], curved in front by the application of steam, 2 inches wide and covered with steel screwed on with wood screws. Jim Simigluak and another native built Dad's sled and, when finished, it was a beauty.

On his first trip to Wainwright, Ned Nusunginya, Dad's driver, told Dad that the sled was pulling hard and he didn't know why. When Dad arrived in Wainwright and settled in at Jim Allen's trading post, he told Jim what Ned had said about the new sled. "We'll bring it into the store," said Jim.

An expert sled maker by the name of Upicksoun was called in and he walked around the sled, stood on the back runners, got down on his hands and knees and examined the runners in great detail. "I can fix," he said. "Runners too flat, need to be like rocking chair."

Upicksoun removed the steel runners and, with two pieces of hickory obtained from Jim Allen, slightly tapered each one so that the thickest part was in the middle. They were fastened on the existing hickory runners, the steel runners were replaced and the sled was taken out for a test ride with Jim Allen's fine team. Eight boys and girls were put into the sled to equal the weight of a normal load and away they went over the snow. It ran beautifully.

Several years ago my oldest son John and his family were in Bloomington with me, visiting the Mathers Museum at Indiana University. I showed him the two strips of extra wood and told him the story.

### Reindeer Herding

*In 1890 Sheldon Jackson, Presbyterian missionary and General Agent for Education for the Alaskan Territory engineered a plan for the importation of reindeer to the state for management by the Iñupiat people. Originally designed to insure that the Iñupiat people would never again have to face starvation, the plan was designed to train apprentice herders, create a system for future individual ownership, provide herds of 'starter' deer, and import Chukchi herders from Siberia to give instruction on animal husbandry.*

*Later in that decade the plan was put into action and a herd was driven to Barrow. Although the primary goal was to provide nourishment for a crew of stranded whalers living there, the herd ultimately benefited the Iñupiat people who owned the herd through a share system. With the assis-*

*tance of Thomas Lopp, the deer were driven to Barrow from Teller on Alaska's western coast, arriving in the spring 1897. Over several hundred deer made it to Barrow and were the beginnings of the village herd. The plan for reindeer evolved up the western coast of Alaska and across the North Slope with varied success among these traditional hunting and gathering people. Although the plan may have been ultimately flawed by the fact that the Iñupiat people were not pastoralists, the herd grew and fed the village for several decades.[40]*

*Although the Barrow village herd was manned by young, single men for several decades, the herd was plagued by poor health and loss due to mixing with wild caribou. The Browers of Barrow developed a herd separate from the village herd with which they were successful, profiting well from business associated with it.*

When I was a boy in Barrow, reindeer meat was our basic food. We ate deer meat in various forms twice a day and to me it tasted like beef. There were two reindeer herds kept around the area. The village owned a herd which numbered between 1,500 and 2,000 head. Young men served as herders, usually four or five in a rotation, and they were paid with deer from the herd.

When they brought the deer into the village, we'd have a big time of butchering them and lassoing and so forth. You never heard so much noise from deer as you did when they were in that village. The deer stayed on the sand around the lagoon and the herders used herding dogs to help contain them. And everybody turned out for that. You decided how many deer you needed and, of course, the skins belonged to you too. When the butchering took place once a year, only the males were shot and killed. The females were permitted to live and reproduce.

Mr. Brower had his own family herd, run by Tom Brower. Tommy had a special place up there by a lake at Alaktak, quite a distance from Barrow where he built a house and lived there with his family. He even did his

*The reindeer were our main source of fresh meat. My father paid Tommy Brower 10 cents a pound for a dressed carcass.*

butchering up there; I can't ever remember him bringing his herd into the village. Dad bought his reindeer meat from Tom at ten cents a pound for a dressed carcass. Dad didn't get the skins. If we ever needed skins, there was no problem getting them. Tommy's was the best meat, his deer seemed to be fatter and in better shape than the village herd. Ten cents a pound, you can't beat that.

# CHAPTER SIX
# THE MISSION'S WORK

*Up-to-date technology was a saving grace for the Arctic-bound missionary. Air travel enabled the sick to be flown out and direly needed supplies to be flown in. Radio service enabled Dr. Greist to serve a greater audience when preaching and expedited calls for medical service. There were also mechanized tools that were used to ease the heavy burden of work needed to keep a hospital and church supplied and functioning.*

### THE FORDSON TRACTOR

*Described by Dr. Greist as "one of the greatest blessings enjoyed by Barrow Mission, material in nature"* (Greist 1/1933:52), *the Fordson tractor enabled the Greists and their helpers to travel great distance while doing their work. In enabled them to transport patients great distances in relative comfort and warmth. Although maintaining such equipment in the Far North was far from easy, the tractor, driven by David and Lee Suvlu, made life easier (and more comfortable) for the traveling missionaries.*

The Fordson full-crawler tractor was there in 1929 when we got back. They had burned out the bearings in it. When the oil got too thick it was so hard to start, so they just drained out all the oil and ran it without. Mr. Morgan poured new bearings for it and we got it running again. The mission was blessed with that tractor which

*Lee Suvlu on the Fordson with a fresh supply of ice for drinking and laundry.*

enabled us to accomplish tasks that previously proved burdensome in the extreme, quickly and efficiently. We also used it to go down the coast on picnics, to go inland for hunting geese and so forth. We used it as part of an ambulance to go down to Wainwright and back. The tractor was just a workhorse.

Dad built two great big 16 foot sleds to pull behind the tractor. We hauled our year's supply of freight (food stuffs, gasoline in 50 gallon drums, lumber and coal) from the beach to the hospital and mission. We used them to go to the post office to get our parcel post every summer. Ice, from which all drinking water and laundry water materialized was hauled as needed throughout the bitterly cold winter months from its storage upon the banks of a small freshwater lake some three miles south of the village. In the summer we'd put empty barrels on the sleds, go out to the lake, fill them up with water for laundry from the same lake and haul the water back to the hospital. We didn't drink it because it had bugs in it, bacteria I think. I think Dad told us not to drink the water we hauled in, but the natives drank it. Our drinking water was from ice. There was a lake up the coast near Shooting Station that we drank from; it was supposed to be good water.

Lee Suvlu and I took turns driving the tractor on these occasions. We started it with a crank on a gasoline tank. After the engine warmed up we switched to the kerosene tank. Once, Lee, Helen and I drove it some 60 miles inland to the butchering of reindeer, called a round-up, and brought back forty-three carcasses weighing approximately 2 tons.

### ARCTIC AMBULANCE

*Early in February of 1934, a messenger arrived by dog team from Wainwright with an urgent message to Dr. Greist that a young Eskimo, Sheldon Segevan, was seriously ill. Miss Tiber, the government public health nurse, was unable to diagnose the ailment, was unable to help the boy, and asked that Dr. Greist come as quickly as he could. The nurse further stated that Sheldon would probably have to be hospitalized.*

The weather was bitterly cold, -43 degrees and growing colder. February winds were fierce. There was drifting snow and the outlook for travel was anything but pleasant. By orders from Dad, Lee and I got the tractor ready and loaded the big 16 foot supply with all the equipment we would need for the trip. Dad had the boys—Lee Suvlu, Woodrow Isaiah, Rex Ahvakana, and Clyde Numnik—build an ambulance. A shelter was built on top of a regular dog sled—a frame of wood covered tightly with canvas. Inside was a spring mattress resting on top of winter deerskins, which have long thick hair. The same kinds of skins were also used for bedding. This contraption was original. The first and only sled ambulance ever built in the Arctic.

Ned Nusunginya was selected to pull the ambulance with a team of thirteen dogs. The caravan consisted of the Fordson tractor with the 16 foot supply sled, which contained oil, drums of gasoline, dog food, sleeping bags, personal items and food. Following this was the 14 foot tent sled upon which was mounted a double white tent. Inside were cots, a cooking stove, bedding, cooking utensils, food stuffs, and a heavy carpeting of reindeer skins. Behind that was my father's dog sled, and, following behind, Ned and the sled ambulance. Chained to the big sled were my nine dogs to be used in the event of tractor breakdown when they would be hitched to Dad's sled so one of us could drive him on to Wainwright. The crew of the caravan consisted of Ned (the ambulance driver), Lee and myself to drive the tractor, Dad and Miss Jenny Brower[41], the daughter of Charles Brower and a fine registered nurse who had received extensive medical training at the University of Southern California.

We left Barrow at 2:00 p.m. on March 3rd with the temperature hovering at -39 degrees. The entire village saw us off. Such a strange montage of vehicles had never been seen before.

We averaged 8 miles per hour when the going was good. We traveled mostly on the frozen sea not far from the beach, but at times we went far out to sea for a better trail.

*Artic caravan starting on the 110 mile journey to Wainwright.*

Lee and I took turns driving the tractor. It was bitterly cold sitting on top of that monster without shelter or heat. After about 2 hours, we would go into the warm tent sled, thaw out and drink a hot liquid (cocoa for me, coffee for Lee) prepared by Jenny. Driving a dog team, one can run along side to keep warm and encourage circulation, but not so on a tractor!

Since we left Barrow so late we did not get very far that first night, probably 30 miles down the coast. We had to carefully pick our way over the ice which was smooth most the time. There were heavy snow drifts which were easily navigated with the Fordson—according to Jenny, however, the equipment and bedding in the tent were tossed in all directions, the occupants of the tent tumbling about from the violent jerking of the tractor. Spilled coffee and stew was accepted in good humor. We did not use tow bars between the tractor and sleds. Instead we used 1 inch ropes, lines as the sailors call them. It was difficult to keep the lines taught, thus the jerking motions that Jenny and Dad had to endure.

We camped the first night opposite the shelter cabin, a government-built traveler's rest house on the beach. It was a two-room affair, one with thirteen stalls for dogs and the adjacent for the travelers. We did not use this, as we had our comfortable tent sled. While Jenny was preparing supper, Lee and I walked up to the cabin. Inside on the wall was a painting of the ship *Trader,* by some unknown artist, trading with the natives along the coast of Nome. On the floor I picked up a loaded 12 gauge shot gun shell which I carried back with me. We found nothing more of interest so we walked back to camp.

Jenny was an excellent cook and her reindeer steaks prepared under adverse circumstances were worthy of long remembrance. After supper we all went to bed, each in his own reindeer sleeping bag, side by side like sardines on the tent floor, sleeping excellently well.

The next morning while breakfast was being prepared, Lee and I placed two kerosene Primus stoves beneath the tractor crankcase to warm up the oil so we could readily crank and start the engine. Lee had sustained a beautiful black eye the previous year when the engine backfired and caught him in the eye. He learned a lesson the hard way. We always start the engine on gasoline (the Fordson had two fuel tanks). After the engine warmed up, we would switch to the tank with kerosene. It would run smoothly all day on kerosene.[42]

After we left the village, I turned the dogs loose. They trotted along side the sleds, occasionally wandering off on the ice to explore, but always returning to the caravan. On the second day we hitched the ambulance sled behind Dad's sled and Ned turned his dogs loose. My dogs had two or three fights with his, but otherwise all went well. The dogs enjoyed this trip because they did not always have to pull a sled. They ran along side the caravan and at night slept tethered to the big sled.

The second night, we camped on Peard Bay which is 20 miles wide and adjacent to the Arctic Ocean. The bay was solid smooth ice over which we made good time. The dogs were too busy keeping up with our 8 mile per hour speed to get into fights.

The third day, we had radiator problems—even with anti-freeze the radiator froze up at -40 degrees. With hot water we thawed it out and replaced the anti-freeze with alcohol (5 gallons which we had on the supply sled). This, in turn, did not protect the radiator so we finally resorted to kerosene and this proved to be satisfactory, serving us well at -45 degrees. It would get thick like molasses at -60 degrees, but would not freeze.

Before reaching Wainwright the third day, it became quite dark. We wished to reach our destination that night so Ned and I took turns dog trotting in front of the tractor with a Coleman gasoline lantern with Lee on 'Old Ironsides' behind us. We reached Wainwright at 9:00 p.m.

The natives knew we were in the proximity because of the tractor noise—the tractor has no muffler therefore one could hear it for several miles.

Dick Hall, a white trader, greeted us and invited Dad and me to stay at his trading post. Jenny enjoyed the hospitality of Mrs. Jim Allen; Jim was outside at the time. Dick Hall had a fine supper prepared—reindeer steaks, fried potatoes, three kinds of canned vegetables, hot biscuits, strawberry jam and homemade Hire's root beer. What a meal after so long a trip in the cold. Additionally, this was my first root beer and I thought it was great!

We stayed in Wainwright for three days. Dad found Sheldon to be a very sick man. He and Jenny got the patient in condition to travel and on Sunday Dad held church service in the schoolhouse as no church had yet been built.

Then we left for home. The ambulance, with Sheldon inside, hitched to the caravan much of the time, saving when rough trails necessitated the use of dogs. Returning to Barrow the number in our company had grown. Now there was Sheldon, his wife, his boy, his brother, Ned, Lee, Dad, Jenny, and myself plus twenty-two dogs.

We made it back to Barrow in three days, arriving there in the afternoon. Most of the village was out to greet us. Thanks to Miss Brower the patient was brought to the hospital in fair condition, his every need on the return trail being cared for almost as well as if he had been in a ward. He was admitted to the hospital where, with proper medical treatment by Dad and my mother, he recovered in fine shape and was able to return to his home in Wainwright three weeks later.

## ROOT BEER & GINGER ALE

Dick Hall knew how much I liked the root beer so he gave me his last four bottles prior to our departure. I placed them all in my sleeping bag but, alas, at -40 degrees I found them that first night frozen, a mess of broken glass and ice which I had to dump out on the snow. Everyone had a good laugh at my expense.

Unbeknownst to me, Dad had learned from Dick Hall where to order a home bottling outfit. That summer[43] Dad presented me with all the equipment with which to make root beer. To bottle the Hire's, I collected empty beer bottles from Mr. Hopson and Mr. Brower.

Julia and I became experts at making root beer. We used a copper double boiler with sugar and yeast, making 5 gallons at a time. After capping, the bottles were placed in a warm place usually behind the cook stoves to activate the carbonation.

All our teenage friends enjoyed this new found drink. My Eskimo chum, Woodrow, one time could not wait for me to find a bottle opener so he removed the cap with his teeth. Prior to this the only soda pop we ever had access to was from the ships that came up each summer—the canteen or ship's store on the USRC Northland would sell us soda pop for a nickel.

Now we had our own supply. When I left Barrow to go to boarding school in Stony Brook, I turned over the bottling business to Julia. To this day I and my sons, Jim and John, are very fond of root beer.

My father and I were down in Wainwright one winter. We were probably on the tractor at the time and we were going to be there for a several days. One day Jim Allen said, "David, I'm sending Sheldon up to the Baychimo[44] camp to bring back a load of coal. Would you like to take my team?" Jim Allen had the best team in Wainwright, a real fast team. So Sheldon and I went up to the camp which was, I think, 25-30 miles up the coast at Peard Bay. The old Baychimo camp was still there. It had been built by men from the ship with lumber and equipment from the ship before it disappeared (see *Ghost Ship of the Arctic: the Baychimo*). Inside the shelter were several bunks where the men had been sleeping and under one of the bunks I found a big bottle of Canada Dry ginger ale. It had frozen and burst open and so I melted the ginger ale in a pan, fished out all the glass and had myself a drink of ginger ale.

We loaded our sleds the next morning to go back to Wainwright. On the way back Sheldon was heading the teams and as I was behind with Jim Allen's team. I was sitting on the sled watching the team and the snow, and every once in a while I'd see a brown spot on the snow where the snow was otherwise white. I asked Sheldon what those brown spots were on the snow and he said, "Oh, I'm chewing tobacco." I got a big charge out of that.

## MEASLES

*The tragedy of epidemics was a hard cross for medical missionaries to bear. Faced with a limited supply of medicine, a society with impoverished immune systems and a shortage of staff to manage the sick, an epidemic of influenza or measles could decimate a village if not stifled quickly and efficiently. The Greists themselves, even young David who was raised away from mainstream culture's germs, escaped danger, but those around them suffered from time to time with maladies otherwise curable elsewhere in the world.*

*Infant paralysis, tuberculosis, typhoid, diphtheria, and measles all claimed victims during the Greists' term, but advancements against the diseases continued to be incremental and beneficial. By 1930 antitoxin serum was shipped north to fight diphtheria. Ultraviolet lamps were used in winter to rehabilitate tuberculosis patients and the Germantown church of Philadelphia donated supplies to build a porch on the hospital so that tuberculosis patients could convalesce in the sun and fresh air of summer. Although the wars against such diseases were never won, the battles were often positive.*

Prior to our arrival in Barrow, a tragic epidemic of measles occurred in 1901. During that year 126 died from the disease. Many panic stricken families escaped to the hinterland and the far Eastward, not one of whom was ever heard from again. They were completely wiped out, probably dying from the disease or starvation or both.

There being no hospital or doctor in Barrow at that time, it was impossible to force the victims to remain within their homes. Practically all fatalities resulted from exposure to the elements and consequent pneumonia which, after measles, is fatal. Charles D. Brower, the white trader at Barrow, did all he could to encourage the natives to remain inside but to no avail. He told my father, "Natives would run a high fever and then they would go outdoors at -40 degrees to cool off." Mr. Brower lost his first wife in that epidemic.

In 1934 a woman and her two children, returning from the states in May, had somewhere along the line, either on board the ship, train or plane, come in contact with the measles. Soon after they arrived in Barrow, the two little girls developed the disease. Not since the fatal epidemic in 1901 had measles been within Barrow.

My father, in cooperation with J.R. Trindle, in charge of the government schools, inaugurated an emergency hospital within the schoolhouse. By strict and energetic measures Dad was able to limit the cases to six and with no fatalities.

Lee Suvlu was told by his mother that he had had the measles in 1901. Since I had had the measles in 1926, he and I were the only two who moved patients, carried supplies and fuel, water and ice to the emergency hospital. I escaped trouble, but not so Lee.

Immediately after dismissing the last case from the schoolhouse, my father felt it was necessary to go to Wainwright, fearing that certain parties who had left for that village might develop the disease and spread it. There was no nurse or doctor in Wainwright at that time. Dad felt a degree of responsibility and so we assembled our caravan—tractor, big sled, tent sled and Dad's dog sled plus all my dogs and off we went. Lee and I took turns driving, arriving in Wainwright in 3 days. Guess who came down with the measles? Lee, of course, and guess who had to drive the tractor 110 miles back to Barrow? I did! Within a very few hours we left Wainwright for Barrow, not wanting to expose Lee's condition to the natives of this small village.

I drove the tractor. Lee, being a very sick man, was put deeply within a reindeer sleeping bag with heavy skins under him. With blankets on top a degree of warmth was maintained throughout the exceedingly cold and windy trip home. Lee suffered no ill consequences and eventually made a good recovery.

Driving the tractor over the ice and snow with the temperature at -46 degrees was not a pleasant task. I had to stop several times and come into the warm tent to unfreeze my hands, feet and nose. While in my tent I also teased Lee in Eskimo as to his comfort in the bag and enjoying the trip in a warm tent.

During that day, my father sat on a chair on the platform in front of the tent sled with a 410 gauge Stevens shot gun. When I appeared to be falling asleep and leaning toward one of the caterpillar treads[45], he would fire the gun in the air and everyone in the caravan including me became suddenly wide awake. This went on for 3 days with no mishap.

After we got home I had Julia, our house girl, feed and tie up my dogs and I went to bed for 14 hours.

INSANITY

*At a time when communication with the outside world was sparse and a community's self-sufficiency was mandatory, infractions of a community's social order were dealt with on a very local level. United States Commissioners were assigned around the state, local citizens who served as marshal-style agents for the government. These individuals assumed the responsibility of settling disputes, reprimanding criminals and otherwise promoting peaceful relations among local citizens. In Barrow, Charles Brower was the United States Commissioner to whom all disputes were taken.*

*If a crime such as theft, assault, or murder occurred in the village, it was his job to deal with the situation in the name of the law. If the Commissioner was away from the village and trouble occurred, community members often had no recourse but to take matters into their own hands. On one such occasion, Dr. Greist took charge.*

In late years insanity apparently increased and, although the cause was not easy to solve, syphilis undoubtedly played a major role. My father observed six cases of such insanity within the Point Barrow district.

There was one tragic example of insanity, that of Willard, a 20 year old Eskimo man. His elderly mother, who was beautiful as a young girl, was very popular with white whalers. She contracted syphilis and later married and raised a family of three boys and two girls. The three boys were tubercular and two went insane. Her children possessed anything but good health, not only being tubercular but neurotic.

Willard was an irritable and unruly son. He continually intimidated his mother and sisters. He frequently exhibited fits of violent temper, threatening bodily harm to anyone he came in contact with. One cold morning Willard removed all of his clothing and, stark naked, climbed on the roof of his mother's igloo armed with a Winchester rifle and a box of ammunition. He claimed he was going to kill all of the men in the village and establish an immense harem. By guile, an older man secured possession of the rifle, and, near frozen, Willard was carried down into the igloo and thawed out.

Later in the week he attempted to burn our Presbyterian church down. My father called the elderly men of the church together and, straight from the shoulder, told them emphatically that something had to be done at once.

First they found an abandoned igloo in which was placed a stove and a solidly constructed bed. Willard was placed inside and was guarded in his new home on a rotation basis by young men in the village. My father supplied

*Willard being taken to Pt. Hope where he was placed in jail—Bert and Bud behind the sled.*

all the meals and coal. All went well for a few days until Willard jumped through a closed window sash, glass and all. My father responded to an urgent call, dressed his wounds and reprimanded him.

Within a week he smashed his bed to bits and, with a short 2 x 4 club, attacked the guards. A terrific fight resulted in that small room and eventually Willard was floored with a blow to the head. Again my father was called to the scene of destruction to dress wounds on both Willard and the guards. My father found a pair of steel handcuffs in the old manse, a strange find within a mission house. He put them on Willard and chained him to a wall. At this time there was no wireless or other facility for rapid communication to the outside. A letter with a native carrier with a dog team would take weeks. The young men were balking against further guard duty, for they were afraid of Willard.

With Mr. Brower being outside, it was decided that Willard should be taken down the coast to Point Hope, some 400 miles away, where the nearest United States Commissioner, the Rev. William Thomas was located. All natives and whites agreed that this should be done, but by whom? No one in the village, Eskimo or white, would volunteer. To make a long story short, my father agreed to take Willard south.

Two men were employed to go, Bert Panigeo, aged perhaps 40 years, a very capable and trustworthy Eskimo and a younger man, Bud Simigluak. Each furnished a fifteen dog team, meat for their dogs and their own sleeping bags. My father supplied everything else.

Many reindeer steaks were frozen and placed in empty flour sacks. A reindeer stew was prepared, poured into trays, frozen and then broken up in pieces the size of your hand. These would be thawed out as needed in a skillet on a small kerosene burning Primus stove. Hot tea and hard tack rounded out each meal.

The dog sled on which Dad rode contained his medical kit, all rifles, axes and knives. Willard was handcuffed to the front sled, one wrist being free. Morose, angry, and grumbling most of the time, he occasionally brightened up and, to all appearances, seemed normal.

Once, he spoke to Dad quietly and kindly begged him to release him so he might have freedom of motion, claiming he was cramped and cold. Dad made the mistake of giving in to his request. Once released, Willard took off out to the frozen sea, dodging ice hummocks as large as single car garages. After a long chase the two Eskimo drivers succeeded in catching him and brought him back, fighting, biting, kicking, cursing and frothing at the mouth. Dad again put him in irons.

Traveling was slow. Daylight came at 10 a.m. and then but feebly. Darkness came with 2 p.m. for this was early March. Six hours a day of travel netted them but 20 miles. Normally a dog team can cover 50 miles a day. It was bitterly cold, the mercury hovering at near -50.

One night the caravan found a deserted trapper's cabin in which they stayed overnight. The two men brought in the "grub box" pumped up and lighted the two Primus stoves (a feat at -50). Then they went outside and fed the thirty dogs, removed them from the harnesses and tied them up with chains.

My father placed Willard on a box in the far corner, easily observed by Dad while he prepared supper for all. He made coffee, thawed out bread, heated up a pot of stew and fried quantities of bacon. Fats are needed when traveling in Arctic temperatures. "Doctor Greist, will you remove these cuffs so I can stretch my arms? I will be a good boy and stay right here where you can watch me," Willard said in a normal tone and with a smile. Dad went to him and removed the cuffs warning Willard to remain in the corner. Dad was wearing his parka of reindeer fur with the hood over his ears and partially over his face for the room was yet very cold, his breath hissing as a fog around him.

The coffee pot boiled over while Dad was slicing frozen bacon and he quickly dropped his large hunting knife and turned to remove the coffee pot. Out of the corner of his eye he saw a hand pick up the knife. Dad turned and instantly grabbed Willard's arm as he was getting ready to plunge the knife into Dad's back. Willard had stealthily crossed the room when he saw Dad engaged with the boiled coffee. Dad shouted for help and Bert came running. Willard fought like a tiger, savagely with eyes blazing defiance. The insane lad was too much for both of them and it was then that Dad shouted for Bud. The three of them finally floored him, but only after Dad had tripped him up. Then jumping upon his breast, pinning his arms to the floor and forcing all the air out of his lungs, Bert Panigeo conquered him.

They handcuffed him with his arms behind his back for the rest of the night and fed him like a baby. Dad slept little that night, watching him with a lit lantern nearby. Willard was pretty well knocked out, having been inoculated with heavy medication.

Needless to say Willard was never turned loose the rest of the trip. Not only did they cuff him with hands behind his back, they also lashed his legs together.

On one other occasion in a deserted cabin Dad had given Willard a hypodermic of medication but Willard fought sleep all night. He got on his knees and swayed to and fro the entire night, mumbling to himself, his eyes fixed on Dad's Colt six gun which he wore day and night in a holster. It was another sleepless night for Dad. The two mushers slept peacefully.

A few days later a terrible blizzard kept them from traveling. It happened at Icy Cape and for two days and nights they were the guests of Upicksoun and his kindly wife. During this time they had little trouble with Willard, although he was guarded day and night.

On the nineteenth day from Barrow they drove into Point Hope or Tigara and up to the front of the Episcopal Mission. Dad stumbled through deep drifts to the outer door and knocked. When the Rev. Mr. Thomas opened the door, he threw his arms around Dad who had frost on his face, snow on his parka, glasses covered with deep rime and hugged him tightly saying, "Oh, Dr. Greist, I am so glad to see you, though I am greatly surprised. Where on earth did you come from?"

Dad explained all. Rev. Mr. Thomas took over, found comfortable quarters for the mushers and placed Willard in jail. Supper was prepared for everyone.

Dad was told that Willard behaved himself and was, in the spring, taken to Oregon where the United States government had a contract with a private institution for Alaska's insane. Two years later when Dad went to the states on leave, he learned that Willard had died from tuberculosis.

While at Point Hope, Dad delivered Mrs. Thomas of a boy. The delivery was difficult, a high forceps one. Dad always carried his obstetric instruments and surgical bag.

Dad spent Easter with the Thomases and even baptized the little boy he had delivered.

He left for Barrow soon after; he had been gone 8 weeks. My Mother and I and the entire village received Dad with open arms.

Dad settled with Bert and Bud, paying them $400. He also paid Reverend Thomas for supplies to cover the return trip. The total amount came to a little over $1,000. Dad sent the bill to the Board of Missions in New York and, much to his surprise, he received in return a letter from his chief stating that the Board could not bear the expense. It would come out of Dad's salary which, at that time, was $1,500 a year. This, of course, stunned Dad; however, this story had a happy ending.

Later when Dad went to the states on furlough he stopped in Nome and paid his respects to the United States Marshall who had arranged Willard's transfer to Oregon. "Did you get your pay?" he asked. "No," Dad replied with the rest of the story. The Marshall looked at Dad sternly and said, "Come with me." He took Dad to the Federal Court House, to the Clerk of the Court and then to the judge. In short, checks were made out to Dad covering the wages of the mushers, all supplies, his mileage to and from Point Hope, his per diem and any and all incidentals. Dad was also made a United States Marshall retroactively. The incident was a lifesaver for our family. Dad went to a store and bought Mother a dress, me a shirt and a toy. He also bought himself a new shirt.

## ORION

Dad was returning from another journey to Wainwright in November during one of the coldest and darkest months of the year. Because of rough ice along the coast, Ned Nusunginya[46] elected to travel on the frozen, snow-covered tundra parallel to the coast, but 5 to 6 miles inland.

After the third day Dad asked Ned to stop the team. "Ned, I think we're going the wrong way."

"No, Dr. Greist, we are going toward Barrow," Ned replied.

"Ned, let me check the compass." Dad got off the sled and went 50 feet away—to get away from the sled's steel runners—and set the compass on a chunk of snow.

"Look Ned, we are traveling East. Look at the compass."

"No, Dr. Greist, that thing is no good. Look at the drifts of snow. We are going to Barrow."

"All right, Ned, let's have a prayer for God's help and I'll get back on the sled." Dad got back on the sled and on they went. The only lights were the northern lights reflecting on the snow. The sky had been overcast since they left Wainwright.

As they moved along Dad was looking at the sky and northern lights when a small opening in the overcast revealed a bright star. A few minutes later the opening got larger and another star was right under the first. Finally, a third star was under the second. There were three stars on a row—the belt of Orion.

"Ned, look at that. You know the stars. That's Orion and, at this time of the year, it is in the East."

"Yes, Dr. Greist stars don't lie." And with that Ned called 'Haw!' to the lead dog and he turned 45 degrees to the left. They arrived in Barrow 2 days before Thanksgiving, tired and hungry. Answer to prayer? The providence of God? I would say yes.

## BEAR ATTACK

A dog team pulled up in front of our house one dark day in the early spring of 1931 after a long and difficult trip from 200 miles to the Eastward. On the sled was a little 10 year old girl whom the father and dog team driver said was "plenty sick."

Dad immediately rushed them to the hospital 100 yards away and, with the help of Helen and my mother, removed the girl's soiled fur parka with much difficulty. The girl's head was terribly matted with blood and soaked hair. Pus was oozing out of a wound together with sand and gravel intermixed. Not only was her scalp and long hair fouled, but also her face and neck. It was a sickening sight. Through an interpreter Dad gleaned this account:

"Me and girl outside igloo near big ice on beach when polar bear came on fast and with big paw tear hair off head. Me shoot quick, kill bear, but girl bleed bad. Me pick up hair from beach and put back on head. We go inside igloo quick. Wife sew hair back on head with sinew. Girl plenty sick. So we pack sled and come quick to Dr. Greist."

Dad and Mother found gravel and sand not only on the scalp mixed with blood and pus but there was also gravel under the scalp.

They cut away the mass of long hair tangled and filthy, cleaning the child's head as best they could with warm soap suds under anesthesia. Dad dissected out the underlying gravel as best he could and then decided to remove the scalp. The mother and father had replaced the scalp irregularly and, therefore, Dad felt he should remove it and replace it correctly. Dad removed the scalp, cleaned out all the gravel and reattached it using cat gut sutures.

Dad and Mother had little hope of the tiny sufferer, but incredible as it may seem she made a good recovery and was able to return to the east with her parents. Prior to their departure Dad baptized the girl and gave her the name Rebecca.

# CHAPTER SEVEN
# HOME

*I*t was during the holidays that the white community *reenacted, Arctic-style, small vignettes from their former world. Flag waving and picnics marked the Fourth of July. Additionally there would be foot races and kayak races, matches of rifle marksmanship and physical feats. Decoration Day, celebrated on Independence Day instead of Memorial Day due to snow being too deep in the cemetery, caused occasion for the children to be instructed on grave decoration, artificial flowers having been saved from the mission boxes. On Halloween, masks were made and parties were given. School children dressed in costumes and the girls of the mission made mince pies.*

*At Thanksgiving a large goose—or the occasional, imported turkey—dinner was consumed by Barrow's white families around a large, festively-decorated table whose centerpiece consisted of a picture cut-out of celery or some other sorely-missed vegetable. Thanksgiving was also a time when the Native population convened for a night of dancing. These dances were encouraged by the teachers and tolerated by Dr. Greist, who did not approve of the events but did not raise a commotion at their occurrence since they were "rather infrequent and did not extend later than reasonable hours."*
(Greist, 12/1931:66)

## CHRISTMAS IN BARROW

*Christmas was the pinnacle of the holiday round. Whether for themselves, far from loved ones and things familiar, or for those they hoped to teach the Christian way, the missionaries squeezed the Yuletide for all of its religious worth. Regardless of the fact that they were hundreds of miles above the tree line, they made and decorated a man-made tree. And, although most of the villagers lacked either the resources or the seasonally-driven motivation to extend gifts to their family and friends, the missionaries made sure that everyone in the village had a gift under the tree. The children received candy and everyone received new clothing or other objects from the mission boxes sent from church members in the lower 48 states.*

*A Christmas dinner for the white families was hosted by one white household or another and Stanley Morgan would bring telegrams to read after dinner. Barrow's Native population celebrated with festivities at the church and one or two nights of dancing at the school.* (Greist, 12/1931:72)

*Santa Claus always made an appearance at the Christmas Eve festivities, courtesy of a village volunteer. Dr. Greist once mused that Santa "must live hard by, since he knows the Eskimo language so very well. He talks to the older people in their native tongue and then at once turns to the young people and the kiddies and speaks in the English language."* (Greist, 1/1931:14)

Because there are no trees in Barrow, we were some 400 miles north of the tree line, our Christmas tree consisted of two 16 foot 2 x 4's fastened together with holes drilled into them at intervals and sticks placed in the holes to resemble branches. The tree was decorated with home-made colored objects made by the school children, but there were no lights as we did not yet have electricity. When done it was a good imitation of a fir tree. We placed it on a rigid platform in one end of the church. The villagers brought their personal gifts for others and laid them on the platform under the "tree" just like one great family.

The native gifts were homemade oars, paddles for kayaks, skins for making boots, in-soles, meat, flour and many odd articles useful to the Eskimo but not sold in markets in the States. The natives were not forgetful of each other at Christmas time; the Yule spirit reigned supreme during the holiday season.

Prior to Christmas, we young people would spend several nights in the hospital kitchen, popping corn and roasting peanuts until we had several tubs full. We opened 200 pounds of hard candy and we evenly divided candy, corn and peanuts into 300 to 400 paper sacks so that each child would have a treat for Christmas. On Christmas Eve a program was given by the children and older ones of the Sunday School. This program was supervised and directed by Mrs. Morgan, Evelyn Komedal, and Lillie Bailey. Later that night we young people would go from house to house singing carols no matter how low the temperature. Afterward we ended up at the hospital for hot cocoa with marshmallows.

In issues of *The Northern Cross,* the Greists would give specific instructions regarding how to wrap and ship donation boxes. Supporters were instructed that mission boxes should be "in cartons, not wooden boxes, the cartons securely wrapped in burlap which is in turn sewed in place, the address written on muslin and sewed upon the box." (Greist 2/1929:48) They were to be shipped via parcel post by June 1st so that they could make the late summer boats. Express or first class mail was unacceptable due to the difficulty or expense of receiving them.

On the previous Fourth of July the MS Patterson would have delivered over a hundred large mission boxes and the candy to the mission. These boxes, sent to us from various churches in the States, also contained a great variety of things: baby clothes, toilet articles, toys, needles, thread, clothes, blankets, talcum powder and so forth.[47] Each November my mother would open and sort out all the goodies with the help of the girls from the hospital.

Baby things went in one pile, toys in another and so forth. Mother would have already compiled a list of every family in the village: names of father and mother, ages and names of the children so that packages could be made accordingly.

Then came the task of making up bushel bags for each family containing something for everyone. They were tied up with the name of the father or mother on each. Absent families in the hinterland trapping or too far away for a visit to Barrow at Yuletide season were not forgotten, their sacks kept in the manse until their return. Come Christmas Eve, the choir sang Christmas music and many gifts were handed out. Dad and Mother were also not forgotten. One year Dad even received two well wrapped frozen fish, some reindeer inner soles and a pair of lovely house slippers made out of reindeer skin. On one occasion I acted the part of old St. Nick and, with much fanfare, I burst into the church. I had my 'wife' with me who appeared lame from the unaccustomed trip. She loudly declared that she would go no further and that she wanted to go back to our reindeer herd, igloo and workshop. This spoken in Eskimo, the audience roared with laughter.

On Christmas Day the natives enjoyed a feast in the church. They brought Eskimo foods of local origin such as walrus, seal and tidbits of whale and *maktak* which they love so well. In addition to this, the mission furnished tea, bread, sugar, hard tack or crackers, rice, and cocoa for the children. All brought their own plates, cups and spoons. While the feast was going on in the church, Dad and Mother were entertaining at the manse. All the whites in Barrow, at that time numbering ten, were treated to a well-prepared goose dinner with homemade biscuits and, for dessert, apple pie made from dried apples, homemade ice cream and coffee. Small gifts were exchanged and, later, wires were read from relatives in the States through the kindness of Sergeant Morgan.

### A Winter's Fire

Let me explain about fires in the Arctic during the time I was a boy. We had no fire stations, no fire hydrants, no running water, and absolutely no way of putting out a serious fire. This is the sad account of our home at Barrow burning to the ground in 1924 as told to me by my mother.

"It was during December, the 19th, during the darkest days of our winter. I was alone with David, two young girls of fourteen and one boy of ten. Ten girls had been at home all evening sewing. At midnight we had finished forty-two dresses to give to other girls at Christmas. Two of the girls stayed the night as it was late and they lived at the other end of the village. The boy was staying to help build fires and do the chores while Dr. Greist was on a medical trip to Wainwright. He was expected back before Christmas.

"The boy slept down stairs, David and I were in the front room upstairs. The girls were in the room next to mine. The fire started in the upstairs storeroom which held everything in the world you could think of. It was so full you could hardly turn around—one hundred or so mission boxes we were going to unpack the next day to get their contents ready for Christmas, our food, clothing, trunks, Christmas decorations, paints, skins, furs, rugs, and at least $1,000 worth of food.

"The fire started at about 7:30 in the morning when smoke and flames awakened one of the girls. She ran into my room yelling, 'FIRE, FIRE house is burning.' I took one look at that room and I realized the hopelessness of it all. The children were so scared I could hardly get the boy started for help. I took a bucket of water upstairs but it might as well have been a teacup full. I shut the doors in the hall upstairs but our rooms were so full of smoke I could not see to rescue personal things.

"The 6 inch ventilator was open and it might as well have been a keyhole. Our windows were built solid and I did not know enough to kick them out. They were double (paned), you know. All was in darkness, I wrapped the bedclothes about David and shoved him downstairs with the girls. We were all choking fearfully. I could find no clothes, and I felt I must go as David was screaming for me and trying to come back. The head of the stairs was at the store room door. I closed the door and went downstairs. There was a light in the living room and I started hunting for the parkas. I got David's on when somebody came in and carried mine out. I found only a sweater and, so in night clothes, sweater and bare feet I began throwing things out of the one door of the house.

"Some help came but the smoke was so bad you couldn't tell white from Eskimo. When I gave an order it was no doubt not understood. Someone spilled a bucket of water on the floor and after 20 minutes I was forced to leave and go to the hospital 100 yards away for clothing. I was terribly cold, shocked and began a nervous chill. The outside temperature was 48 below (zero). I did go back, but I could not enter the house anymore. When the ammunition began going off the workers left the house. They never thought of trying to enter my bedroom by the windows on the other side of the house and save things.

"Most of the weather bureau instruments were saved— I was also the official US Government weather observer. My sewing materials and most of Dr. Greist's theological books were saved, three guns and some surgical instruments and a few tools were also saved. Peter van der Steere, the single school teacher, knew where I kept my good silver and he saved it all. The mission Victrola, a good office chair, two rockers and a table were all broken but saved. Two tea kettles and a double boiler were saved from the kitchen. The fire was above the kitchen and all others but myself were afraid to go in there. It was dark in there, but I knew where they were and I made two men carry out my big ice and water tank.

"The things that were lost—all my linens, Dr. Greist's microscope, medical books, typewriter, all personal important papers, mission papers, records of church business and the mission money box. Also destroyed was a large trunk filled with curios, raw ivory, cut ivory, skins and a beautiful lot of needlework done by my schoolgirls. I wanted all these things to take out to the states for museums, friends and to exhibits. So many nice clothes had been sent us for traveling home to the States.

"We spent the 20th and 21st in the hospital. Dr. Greist returned from his trip to Wainwright on the 21st at 2:00 p.m. The days were dark and his driver drove the team up to the manse. He had not heard of the fire and when he got off the sled instead of his two story home he saw only a blank, barren and blackened rectangle area. It was an awful shock to him, especially not knowing that we were safe.

"How the fire started, no one knew. The store room had no stoves or flues. There was a carton of matches there and it is possible the cat or the house boy could have started it. The boy denies being near the matches.

"An empty two room house was secured for us and Peter van der Steere was able to put up two stoves in it. People began bringing all of our things that were in the church, school and hospital. The whites in the village gave us canned goods. The hospital gave us four cases of canned milk and 50 pounds of butter. We were able to get flour, sugar and coffee from the trading post. The fire was in December, we had 8 months supply of food burn up, because the next shipment would not be until August when the supply ships came in.

"In the spring Dr. Greist went to the corner of the house where our bedroom had been and sifted through the ashes until after 3 days he found the diamond from my wedding ring. My daughter-in-law, Alicia, was married with that diamond to our David.

"Masu, an Eskimo widow with only one eye, was hired by Dr. Greist to make boots, pants, and parkas for all three of us. She worked day and night and was able to finish them by Christmas. Dr. Greist paid her $20 for her hard work.

"Under the homemade Christmas tree at the church on Christmas day was a 23 pound sack of sugar and a 25 pound sack of flour, each costing $10. Written on the sacks, 'To my missionary from Masu.' Dr. Greist broke down and cried.

"Twenty years later the house boy confessed that he took his bed clothes to the store room that morning by using matches to light the way. He forgot to take the lantern that was always lit and near his cot. He must have thrown a lighted match down in a big bag of raw peanuts which was close to the carton of matches. After the fire that boy went east by dog team and never came back to Barrow for years.

"We survived the rest of the winter and returned to the States the summer of 1925. This was to be our first furlough in 5 years."

When the manse burned to the ground we were all left without clothing, bedding, and food for many months. After the fire we moved down to an empty house and Dad had to scrounge food and stuff from all the different traders and so forth to be replaced by all of his supplies when they arrived in the summer. I don't know what we did for clothes. Of course Dad had just come back from a trip so he had all of his stuff with him. Miss Dakin of the hospital could only let Dad have so much butter and flour and sugar and stuff like that, but we were able to manage all right. I'm sure the coal was in the store house so it didn't burn up and the oil house didn't burn either.

*The burning of the manse was a devastating setback for the mission at Barrow. Not only did the fire threaten the lives of those immediately dwelling within, but also those who would have to spend the rest of the winter without their home and belongings.*

*The Greists surely lived a hard winter. Such an event is a telling tale of the sense of community present in arctic villages. With the burning of their home, and supplies not scheduled to arrive for another 7 or 8 months, the Greists could have easily suffered even greater hardship from hunger or cold, but other members of the community came to their aid. They found shelter in an empty frame house and otherwise survived on the credit of their coming supplies and gifts of other necessities, given simply because they were needed. With this one tragedy it became apparent that they were villagers; they had become embedded in the community.*

*The fire perhaps changed David's life most drastically. It was the catalyst that sent him out of Alaska for the first time since his arrival as a toddler. At the age of seven he would have many of his first memorable experiences. The family lived in Alaska for a while and eventually went outside to raise money for a new mission house in Barrow.*

After the manse burned we waited until August when the boats came and went to Nenana for a year. I don't remember much, but I know that we had an earthquake while we lived in Nenana and I learned how to spell the words potato and tomato because I used to have to go down to a neighbor's house to get fresh water. They had the only good well water in town, but before they'd let me have a bucket of water they'd make me learn how to spell potato and tomato.

In Nenana there was a guy by the name of Dixie Hall. He and Mrs. Hall ran the Northern Commercial Company store and they had two boys. I used to play with them. Once in a while, whenever they could, they would have a little picture show in the store. People would come in and sit on boxes of food and stuff and watch the movie, black and white with captions.

Then Dad went on the missionary boat *Princeton,* a boat out of Juneau that belonged to the church. While my father was going up and down the inside passage ministering to the sick, Mother, two Iñupiat girls who had been going to school in the area—Cornelia Phillips and Flossie George, and I rented a house in Juneau. As I remember there were no sidewalks, just steps up to our house because Juneau is built into the side of a mountain. And while we were there I remember Mother taking me to visit Haines House, an orphanage that she had something to do with. They had just built it when we were there. Every once in a while Dad would be able to come home and stay with us for a few days before he went out again.

After that we went back to the States and Dad lectured to raise money for the manse. Mother and I went to Indianapolis and stayed there while Dad lectured all over the United States. We lived in an apartment on Marion Avenue, I think. It was the first time I experienced people delivering milk bottles to your door and I thought that was really something. I also remember that I stood out and watched lightning because I was fascinated. Mother spent time just relaxing and taking care of me. When we left Indianapolis we returned to Barrow.

## The New Manse

Through the lectures he gave and the promotional work he did for an entire year, Dad raised $15,000 to pay for a new manse. Mom, Dad, and I returned to Barrow on the US Revenue Cutter Bear with plans for a new home.

My brother, Wishard,[48] a New York architect and construction engineer of some prominence, drew up the plans for the new manse. He was advised by my father of the peculiar needs and problems of the Arctic. His final blue prints for the new home were of such high quality that they were accepted by the architect of the Board of National Missions in New York without change. Dad went to Seattle and purchased all of the building materials and tools needed for the construction and planned to have them all shipped to Barrow in August.

*The manse, the warmest house in the Artic, built by my dad in 1929. In 2002 it can still be seen in Barrow. The plans were drawn up by my brother Wishard, an architect and engineer from New York City.*

A professional carpenter sent to Barrow for a year would have cost $6,000, so Dad volunteered to not only serve in the capacity of physician and surgeon to the hospital, tend to the several churches, but also don the carpenter's apron and erect the manse upon our return to Barrow in 1929. I helped during construction by running errands, staining all the cedar shakes which hung on the exterior, and picking up all the scrap lumber, nails, and tools left behind after a day's work.

The foundation for the new manse was a challenge. 4 x 4 posts were sunk into the permafrost eighteen inches deep using crow bars and pick axes. Forty-one holes were thus dug and the pillars were cemented in place. When the ship arrived with all the lumber, construction of the structure was begun.

Father selected six or eight Eskimo men from the village, trained them in the proper use of the hammer, saw and chisel and in how to read a measuring tape. They each earned 50 cents an hour.

From August 15th to the middle of October the super structure was accomplished, much of it done in adverse weather conditions.[49] It was an all wooden building; wooden buildings did not deteriorate in the cold, dry climate of the Arctic and many are not even painted. The floor was 24 inches above the ground. The windows were composed of three permanent sashes, each with double panes of glass, the dead air space making for good insulation. A person looked through three panes of glass to the outdoors. The walls were 16 inches thick—the inner wall had Celotex; 2 inch thick Armstrong pressed cork between the studs for insulation; ship lap over the cork; black building paper; and, finally, on the exterior, cedar shingles.

The shingling was the last to go on the exterior, with winter already upon us. Winds blowing a gale, flying snow, and the men dressed in fur parkas and fur boots with faces turned blue and fingers numb, the last green stained shingle was nailed on by December when we moved in. The days were short then with darkness arriving in the early afternoon. The finishing work inside plus painting was accomplished with artificial light provided by Coleman gasoline lamps and heat from the coal burning stove.

It was a two story building with three bedrooms and a store room on the second floor. The store room contained all the canned milk and canned food for an entire year. Twenty pound sacks of flour, sugar and rice plus coffee and tea were stacked in an outside warehouse where freezing was no problem. One bedroom was for my parents, one for me and the third was designated "Nurse's Rest." This took the place of "Nurse's Home" as used by hospitals in the States. It also served as a guest room for infrequent guests.

The first floor contained an unheated entryway where heavy furs could be removed and hung up. Also a gun rack with some ten to fifteen rifles, loaded and ready for use in the event a polar bear should wander by.[50] There was also, on the first floor, an office for my father, a very large living room and a large "country type" kitchen with built-in cabinets, many drawers and counter tops. A large, coal burning Majestic range with warming oven above proved to be a joy for cooking, baking and heating.

A small room behind the range contained a 300 gallon water tank on a high platform. Into this tank I would place large cakes of ice which were melted into hot water by pipes running through the wall into the fire box of the range and then back again. This was the first house in the Arctic to have hot running water.

The bathroom was next to the tank room containing the only bathtub in Barrow; it also enjoyed hot running water. Waste water from the bathtub and sink was drained to the outside through a 2 inch iron pipe. The manse also had a chemical toilet. However, in the small room where the gasoline tank was, Dad had a special bucket where all the men would urinate. He didn't want all of us to use the toilet because that would just fill it up with liquid. He wanted solid matter in there so all the men had to use that bucket. He put a disinfectant in it so it didn't smell at all.

There was a cold, unheated room that acted as a refrigerator. Another unheated room was our coal bin that I kept filled with 1,000 pounds of coal. Five coal burning stoves were designated for the new manse, three upstairs and two down. The house was so well insulated and snugly built that one base burner in the living room was the only one used in all the years we were there. The other heating stoves were never used, not even in sixty below weather.

The guest room upstairs was used by Colonel and Mrs. Lindbergh when they visited us in 1931. My room and the guest room were made ready for Wiley Post and Will Rogers in 1935, but their untimely death near Barrow prevented their use. James A. Ford, archaeologist from the American Museum of Natural History in New York City occupied that guest room for an entire year.

*According to* The Northern Cross *of June 1930, Miss Julia T. Sherman of Buffalo, New York presented the Barrow hospital with "a very splendid electric light outfit ... a two machine plant of 2 kilowatt capacity generators." They arrived on that summer's boat, but while the gift was a blessing, it had a bumpy start. The shipment of equipment contained no bulbs nor oil and the plants generated interference for the local wireless radio until a homemade filter was manufactured. "The plant is sufficient in power to light all buildings of this Mission, but we as yet have insufficient materials with which to wire the premises. Perhaps we may be able to do so another year."* (Greist 1/1931:2) *The church was not wired to receive electricity until 1934.*

*In addition to being able to use ultraviolet lights to "put vitality into convalescents and other cases suited thereto," the use of the electric power plants changed the way business was done around the mission. Dr. Greist praised electricity, commenting, "At present we run the washing machine (belonging to the manse) with a gas engine, but in time we hope for an electric washer." No less were the hospital helpers amazed. "The Eskimo maids think it little less than a miracle, and in an hour can do with it as much labor as formerly called for up to twelve hours hand work."* (Greist 1/1933:56)

To provide light in the mission's buildings, we first had kerosene lamps. When we built the second manse we installed a Coleman gasoline system. In a small room in the manse we had a gasoline tank that you pumped up. Lights hung down from the ceilings of every room with little tubes going to each fixture. You would light each one with a match.

In 1930, we installed an electrical system. A wealthy Presbyterian woman in Buffalo, New York gave my father $2,000 with which to purchase an electric light plant. The two Kohler generators came that summer and Sergeant Stanley Morgan installed them in the hospital. We were blessed with real electric lights.

Mr. Brower had an electric light plant with batteries for a while. He had a big fan on top of his house which charged up all his batteries and he had electric power that way. When we first got to Barrow there was a 32 volt Delco plant in the hospital, but I don't think it was very successful. I don't remember too much about it, but I think it was direct current too. You had to be sure that the wires went to positive-negative not alternating.

Mr. Morgan helped get the hospital's gasoline-fueled generators running and showed Lee how to run and take care of them and so forth. Those generated electricity for the hospital and then the Lindberghs, when they were there, gave enough money to electrify the manse with wiring and light bulbs. Those two plants at the hospital also gave the manse power—mostly lights. Dad also had an ultraviolet ray lamp that he used on, probably, tuberculosis patients. I think he also had some kind of light for his microscope. He would turn them off at night because he didn't see the purpose of running them all night. Everybody had to have their kerosene or gasoline lights ready at 9:00 or 10:00 at night when he decided to shut down the plants. For a year's worth of power it took several 55 gallon drums of gasoline.[51]

### Our Ice House

All drinking water was obtained from melting fresh water ice. When the small, round, fresh water lake a half mile behind Barrow froze over to a thickness of 10 to 12 inches we would go out with a group of men and cut up the ice in 4 by 8 foot slabs. We would then stack the slabs on the lake shore in an upright position, making them easier to separate with an ax throughout the winter. During the winter, Lee and I would go out to the lake with the tractor, pulling 16 foot sleds[52] and dig out the ready cut ice which was now covered with snow. We would cut the slabs into 50 or 60 pound pieces and haul sleds full to the manse and hospital. The pieces were stacked outside

*The ice house. This supplied us with drinking water ice all summer. The manse is in the background.*

each of the hospital and church buildings on long benches, and were carried into the warmth of the kitchens where long, 50 gallon galvanized tanks were kept full.

One of my many chores was to keep the tanks filled with ice; Julia would always inform me when the tanks in the kitchen were getting low. I would shave off any grass or dirt that had gotten onto the ice and chip off pieces which would fit into the tanks. I would then lower the smaller pieces very slowly and carefully, with tongs, so as not to damage the tanks.

Winter time was no problem, but in the summer we had to have some way to keep the slabs of ice from melting. Meat cellars were not large enough to store a summer's supply of ice. My father built a rectangular building half way between the manse and the hospital. It was 18 feet long and 12 feet wide. The roof was covered with sod. It was not a very elegant structure, but the sod served as excellent insulation. Into this house Lee and I stacked ice, filling it to the ceiling and out to the front door as soon as freezing temperatures occurred. When summer arrived and temperatures soared to 45 to 50 degrees we had ample ice from the icehouse for both the manse and the hospital. We did not use the melted ice water for laundry purposes. Instead, Lee and I would hitch up the sleds behind the tractor with empty 50 gallon drums, which we filled from the fresh water lake inland from Barrow a mile or so. This was laundry and dish washing water. In the wintertime we had to use melted ice for these purposes.

### Nature's Deep Freezer

Across Arctic tundra there are no trees or bushes and the summer grass is sparse and brown. This area has a unique quality. During summer the ground thaws about 6 inches and from there on down for a thousand or more feet it is frozen, hard as concrete. You can't pound a one inch stake into it to tie a dog to. I have tried and the rod bent over.

This phenomenon—called permafrost—has given the natives of the Arctic a natural deep freezer for their meat. Every Eskimo family dug a vertical tunnel into this frozen pan for 6 to 10 feet and then carved out a room at the end in which to store fresh meat, fish or fowl. The temperature would not vary more then 5 to 10 degrees, summer and winter staying at -15 to -20 degrees down there. Meat would freeze solid in a matter of hours. A wooden cover over the entrance prevented warm air during the summer from entering the tunnel.

When my father built the mission meat cellar, he made it much larger than most since it was to be used by the hospital also. He blasted a hole with dynamite and shoveled out the resulting pieces of earth. His tunnel went down fifteen feet, and the room at the bottom was at least 20 feet long and 8 feet wide. A wooden ladder reached down to the bottom. Besides a hinged cover, Dad erected a small wooden shed over the tunnel. At the apex of the shed was a heavy duty hook with a block and tackle used to lower carcasses to the bottom where they were hung on hooks in the room. The floors, walls and ceiling were bare permafrost and the only timber used were 4 x 4 inch beams across the ceiling, from which we hung up to fifteen carcasses at one time. In our cellar I had a wooden bench resting on saw horses on which I could place a reindeer and readily saw it into the various cuts of meat needed by our house girl, Julia, or my mother. I did the cutting with an old-fashion meat saw which was used years ago in meat markets and looked like a giant hacksaw. The only illumination I had was from a gasoline Coleman lantern.

I would get the daily required meat order from my mother or Julia which I fulfilled in the morning. The reindeer steaks or roasts would then be placed in the warming oven above our coal burning kitchen range where thawing would take place prior to the evening meal. Besides deer, we had ducks, brant, plover, fish, and ptarmigan down there.

During the summer outside temperatures could range from 40 to 60 degrees above zero. Our summers were 2° to 3 months long. Whenever a death occurred in the summer, the body was lowered into the mission meat cellar until the family of the deceased could dig a proper grave, a task often taking 2 weeks. The body would then be brought up, placed in a home-made coffin which was covered with white canvas, and buried.

As a 12 to 16 year old I was often reluctant to go down into the cellar when I knew what was at the other end of the room. I would beg Julia, who was nineteen, to go with me, but she knew what was down there and, of course, all I ever got was a "no." I would sing, whistle, and try to avert my eyes from looking at the other end. I assure you I did not waste time sawing and securing the required cuts. Later Lee Suvlu and I hung a canvas curtain over the morgue section. That helped, but it did not alleviate my concern.

*My oldest son John coming up out a meat cellar belonging to David Leavitt, Sr. John is an engineer who lives in Miami, Florida, with his family.*

In more recent times, cellars are still used by the natives of Barrow. In 1971 when Alicia and I visited Barrow, I took her down into Tommy Brower's meat cellar.

### Holy Soda Crackers

First class mail came four times during the winter. Ned Nusunginya, the official US Mail carrier would start out from Barrow with his fourteen dogs and sacks of first class mail. He would travel down the coast picking up mail as he visited each village and by the time he reached Point Hope the mail carrier from Nome would meet him and they would exchange mail. Ned would then begin the long journey back to Barrow, dropping off mail on the way. For each trip he received only $75. All parcel post accumulated at Nome until summer, when the cargo ships would deliver bulk mail and packages to the coastal villages. My mother would put in an order to Sears in Seattle in March and we would get delivery in August. Often she would order a pair of blue jeans for me and by the time they arrived I would have already outgrown them.

Besides the parcel post. these ships would bring lumber, coal, gasoline, kerosene and all our food supplies for the next 12 months. Every March my mother and father would make out their requisition for canned goods, sugar, flour, coffee, tea, etc. to the Schwabacker Hardware and Supply Company in Seattle. These things would be loaded on CS Holmes, a four-masted ship under the command of Captain John Backland[53] of Seattle and the ships would arrive usually in August when the coast was free of the ice pack which land-locked us 9 months out of the year. There was a great deal of elation among all of us when the ships arrived for this was our first contact with the outside world in a year. There were no docks at Barrow, so all cargo was brought to shore in small boats and unloaded on the beach. The natives and the ship's crew worked all day and night unloading, for a change in the wind could bring the ice back in and crush the ship. This was a great fear among all ships coming into the Arctic.

From the beach everyone pitched in to move the coal, lumber, foodstuffs etc. to our warehouse or to the manse. My mother took the girls from the hospital who, with rakes, raked in the spilled coal, which had been dumped on the beach, from the edge of the ocean to higher ground. Coal was a precious commodity, costing $60 a ton to Barrow. The girls also prepared a noon-time meal consisting of reindeer stew, bread, and tea for all the freight movers.

All of our perishable items were stored in our house to keep them from freezing during the winter months when temperatures fell to as low as -60 degrees. Items such as gasoline, coal, lumber, sugar, and flour went to the mission warehouse.

On one particular occasion Mother had ordered 200 pounds of soda crackers. During the second day of unloading, Lee Suvlu came to the manse, found my father and said,

"Dr. Greist, what you want me do with crackers?"

"They go into the warehouse, Lee," said Dad.

"No, no, Dr. Greist, too much too many," Lee tried to explain.

"Lee, I said put them in the warehouse!" Dad exclaimed.

"Dr. Greist, you come with me and look," said Lee. So Dad reluctantly followed Lee half a mile down to the beach where all the mission cargo was piled up. "See, Dr. Greist?" What my father saw was quite a shock. Mother had ordered 200 pounds of crackers and someone in Seattle had misread the order and, instead of 200 pounds, had shipped us 200 wooden cases! Each case was the size of an Army footlocker but perhaps not quite as long and weighed about 60 to 80 pounds. There was no use sending them back as all freight delivered to Barrow was $40 a ton. So what to do with so many boxes?

Our church was short of chairs; many of the natives had to sit on the floor. So Dad had all 200 boxes put into the church and they were used as chairs. We had crackers to last us 5 years. In that climate they would not mildew or spoil.

When the Lindberghs visited us in 1931, they attended Dad's church service Sunday morning. We were standing up and I was sharing a hymn book with the Colonel. As we sat down he leaned over and whispered to me, "What are we sitting on?"

"Soda crackers," I said, "I'll explain later."

Just before this lovely couple left to conclude their trip to the Orient, Charles Lindbergh took my father to one side and said, "Dr. Greist, here is a check for $200 for you to buy chairs for the church. I would appreciate it if you would not mention this to the press." The next summer, 1932, the church enjoyed fifty new chairs.

## ARCTIC GROCERIES

*Although the diet of the Iñupiat people prior to heavy western influence was nutritionally narrow, its variety was myriad. Products harvested from the sea—whale, seal, walrus, bearded seal; air—plover, duck, goose, ptarmigan; and tundra—caribou, berries, and other assorted plant material—composed a diet nutritionally sound but alternately plagued with scarcity and abundance. The world of the hunter and gatherer was never a sure thing.*

*For most whites new to the Arctic, adaptation to a high protein, high fat, low roughage diet surely caused some physical and psychological adjustments. While describing the Christmas meal of 1930 in* The Northern Cross, *Mrs. Greist commented that "a beautiful lithograph of a bunch of celery will adorn the center of the table."* (Greist 1/1931:3) *Fresh vegetables were dearly missed.*

*Arriving in Barrow at such a young age, David grew accustomed to the Iñupiaq diet. Due to either taste or professional beliefs, his parents seemed to prefer the food that came to them in their annual shipments from outside. The new tastes of seal oil and raw frozen whale meat gave pause to their new consumers, motivating them to search for new ways in which to capitalize on the annual shipments of food from the lower 48.*

*Prior to air flight, supply ships were the only contact with goods from Seattle and beyond. The journeys were long and prohibited the transport of anything but the most hardy of foods. It was difficult to preserve foods that could not be frozen or those whose shelf life was short. Creative storage methods, such as sleeping with onions, and cooking methods, such as baking apple pies with dried apples, allowed the white population some familiarity at their dinner table.*

The basic food we had at Barrow around which all meals were prepared was reindeer. The reindeer meat would be supplemented with seal liver, goose, duck, and plover— all of which were very tasty when prepared by my mother or Julia. All other food stuffs were tinned. Our annual

*There is no harbor at Barrow. Supply ships anchored off shore and the cargo was transported to the beach in small boats.*

grocery delivery was in July and August. My mother sent in her requisition to Seattle in March and the order would be filled and placed on one of the supply ships coming to Barrow, sailing from Seattle in June.

Flour, sugar, and rice came in bulk. Butter came in barrels of brine and remained fresh for the entire year. Eggs presented a special problem. We would turn the crates over once per week and we would coat each egg in paraffin. We would then pack them in layers of flour in barrels, small end of the egg down, not allowing them to touch each other with each layer covered with flour until the barrel was full. This was a chore that Hester Panikpak, Greta Toovak, Flora Leavitt, and Terza Ungarook—the girls in the hospital kitchen—were given.

Produce presented a problem. Fruits such as apricots, peaches, apples, and prunes came dried in flat wooden boxes. Oranges, lemons and fresh apples could by kept for a short time until all were eaten. The 'fresh' vegetables, when received, would be nearly two months old. We never received bananas, lettuce, cabbage, or fresh peaches.

When crates of potatoes arrived they looked like a giant spider, the crates completely covered with sprouts. The sprouts were removed and the potatoes placed in our meat cellar where they froze hard as rocks. When needed the potatoes were dropped in boiling water and cooked in that fashion. They were much better than dried potatoes.

Although a limited supply of onions would be ordered, their life was limited. Fred Hopson instructed my mother on how to care for them. "If they have sprouts when they arrive, you take the short blade of a knife and push it through the onion just under the sprout from side to side, cutting off the sprout just under the skin. You wiggle your knife sideways and pull out the sprout. You then fold down the outside dry skin of the onion well over the hole. You must now keep them from freezing. You take the onions to bed with you every night, placing then under the comforters and blankets at the foot of the bed where your feet will keep them at the right temperature. In the morning you take the onions to the kitchen and keep them on the floor behind the cook stove."

Slabs of bacon and whole hams arrived every summer very badly molded no matter how well the meat company wrapped them. Mr. Hopson told us to unwrap them, wash them two or three times with soda water then fresh water, dry with a cloth, pepper them all over with plenty of pepper, hang them up from rafters in the attic and leave them there. In time the mold faded away.

In the late 1930s Hormel began canning hams and chickens which were delicious.

Fowl such as ptarmigan, ducks, geese, and brant would be placed in our meat cellars feathers and all without being drawn. For a Sunday dinner, I would bring up two geese on Wednesday. Julia or Terza would hang them up in the kitchen and, by the third day, they would be thawed enough to be plucked and drawn.

The natives soon learned that Dad liked fish. Grayling, tomcod, salmon, trout, and white fish were plentiful in the summer and fall. Fish were no problem when frozen. Dad even said that fresh frozen fish eaten raw tasted like cucumbers. I could neither agree nor disagree because I didn't know what a cucumber was.

Klim powdered milk came to replace Carnation canned milk. After he returned to the States in 1936, my father still preferred canned milk in his coffee to fresh milk or cream.

# CHAPTER EIGHT
## FAMOUS VISITORS

*Although the Native people on the northern coast of Alaska had, from the mid-nineteenth century, constant contact with whalers, traders, and, later, missionaries, they also made contact with the occasional explorer. These visitors from around the globe would arrive and stay for varying lengths of time while they adjusted their plans and replenished their supplies for the next leg of their journey. The Iñupiat people, usually welcoming of strangers coming in from the cold, frequently did not rate even the briefest mention in the explorers' publications and journals.*

*Often these visitors repaid the hospitality of their hosts in Barrow by using some skill to make life easier, better or, at least, entertaining at this isolated outpost. Mechanics fixed things that had long been broken and out of commission. Explorers traveling with well-heeled and tested dog teams left behind sires and mothers for future dogteam leaders. Others, such as Colonel Lindbergh, affected the lives of those in more subtle ways, teaching the children party tricks or leaving behind cherished memories of private interaction. All of those who passed through this crossroads of everywhere, however, made a contribution to the lives of those like David, growing up under unusual conditions.*

*If not merely on their way to or from some other point, these visitors arrived to research or collect pieces of the arctic culture and wildlife. Many pieces of Iñupiat material culture traveled away from the village to museums across the country. Objects were dug from the ground or given up for*

*Lt. Omdal overhauling the Evinrude outboard motor in our kitchen.*

*little or no compensation as new technology came to replace old in this pragmatic society.*[54]

## Lieutenant Omdal

*Norwegian explorer Roald Amundsen made multiple trips to Alaska during his attempts to traverse the North Pole and investigate its presence as a possible land mass by plane. During his second trip in 1922, Oscar Omdal was the pilot of Amundsen's all metal monoplane or junker.*

The famous Arctic explorer Roald Amundsen was contemplating a flight from Barrow across the North Pole and on to Spitzbergen. While he was in Barrow in 1922 and 1923, he and his mechanic Lieutenant Omdal visited us in the manse.

Lieutenant Omdal repaired my wind up Lionel train, my wind up motor boats and fixed my wagon. He also repaired our wall clock. One day when he was in our storage shed he discovered an Evinrude outboard motor. It was quite old with a wooden handle on the fly wheel which was used to rotate the fly wheel to start the motor, later models used a pull rope.

Lieutenant Omdal asked Dad about the motor. Dad explained, "I use it in the summer to push a whale boat to Point Barrow, 12 miles to the northeast, where I hold services Sunday afternoon. It is a pesky thing. My native helpers who go with me sometimes spend an hour trying to start that motor."

Lieutenant Omdal asked Dad if he could look it over. It was brought into the kitchen and placed on the dining room table. There he completely disassembled that motor. He seemed to know what he was doing. He secured some aircraft engine parts which he had on hand. These he modified to fit the Evinrude. At the end of 4 days he had that motor running and purring like a kitten. We had to eat our meals in the living room during that time.

A year prior to this incident Roald Amundsen was giving a lecture on his Arctic experiences to a huge audience in Oslo. Seated in the front row was a renowned sculptor and artist. On his sketch pad he drew several likenesses of Amundsen as he was speaking. Later he carved a pipe out of a piece of fine briar. The front of the bowl had the face and head profile of Amundsen. When finished he presented the pipe to Amundsen. Not wanting to smoke his own face, Amundsen presented the pipe to Lieutenant Omdal who was an avid pipe smoker. Lieutenant Omdal had the pipe with him at Barrow. My father, also a pipe smoker, admired the pipe.

In 1910 my father practiced medicine in Casper, Wyoming. While there he purchased a western type leather belt and holster for his 38 revolver. The holster and belt was the object of many conversations by visiting white men to Barrow. Lieutenant Omdal was no exception. He had never seen such a beautiful belt and holster as this one. Prior to Lieutenant Omdal's departure, Dad presented him with the belt and holster. Lieutenant Omdal remarked to Amundsen, "What in return can I present to the doctor?" Amundsen replied, "You feel embarrassed smoking my face in my presence so why not give the pipe to Dr. Greist." He did so. Both men were happy with the trade. As was true in the North at that time you did not buy or sell, you traded. My father kept that pipe until his death in 1955.

In 1928, the Italian arctic explorer Umberto Nobile started out for the North Pole in a dirigible, the *Italia,* from Spitzbergen. He crashed soon after take off and was believed dead for 6 weeks, but was later found by one of the rescue planes. One of the rescue parties consisted of Amundsen, Omdal and three other men in a plane. They were never heard from again. It was the last arctic expedition for Amundsen. Where they crashed or how they died remains a mystery to this day.

## James A. Ford

*Archaeologist James Ford made significant contributions to the study of Iñupiat prehistory on the North Slope. Visitors with such a specialized scientific purpose exposed David to other ways of thinking. With many of these visitors staying in his home for extended periods of time, they could only have augmented his education and inspired his growing mind. The field trip came to him.*

In the summer of 1932 when I was fourteen, a young man about 6 foot 4 arrived in Barrow on the MS Patterson who, we soon learned, was an archaeologist in his 20's from the American Museum of Natural History in New York City. He camped in a tent about four miles toward Point Barrow and began digging on some ancient home sites. He was quite successful in finding many artifacts relating to the early inhabitants of the region.

Toward the end of summer he approached my father and asked him for room and board for the coming winter. "Why?" asked my father. "I have received permission from my superiors to remain through the winter so that I may begin excavating early in the spring. What would you charge?" $75 per month was agreed upon and James A. Ford moved into my room. We became roommates.

James and my mother hit it off well, for Mother was an amateur archaeologist. She had been sending birds, eggs and artifacts to the museums in Chicago and Indianapolis for years. James instructed Mother in many aspects of archaeology—what the artifacts were used for, what they were made from and how to estimate their ages. Mother was a night person, as was James. They would often sit up at night in our living room by the big base burner reading until 1:00 or 2:00 in the morning.

By the early 1930s the manse's lighting system consisted of gasoline ceiling lamps in all the rooms. They were all connected with small copper tubing to the main gasoline supply tank and pump in the store room.

One evening I went to bed early and I asked, "Ford, you want me to leave the light on?" And he said, "Leave it on. I'll be up in a little while." I went to sleep and an hour later I was awakened by the smell of smoke. James' bed was on fire. This time I yelled for him and he ran into the room, pulled his mattress down the stairs and dragged it out into the -30 degree night. The edge of James' bed had been under the lamp and the gasoline had leaked and dripped. One of the drips had caught fire. The mattress was destroyed. That was a very close call; arctic fires were impossible to put out once out of control. Unless caught early, fire extinguishers were useless.

James adjusted well to winter in Barrow. My mother had some Eskimo women make fur garments for him and they had never made a parka for so tall a man or fur boots for size thirteen feet. He learned to hitch up my dogs and drive the team. He went out on the ice pack to the spring whaling camp. He made a trip to Wainwright by dog team when my father went down.

Early in the spring Ford went back to his digging. I joined him but lasted only one week; I got bored with it.

It was a tedious job and I did not have the patience to excavate as he instructed me. The proper method was to scrape one inch of dirt off the top at a time. Hour after hour we did this. If you found something you couldn't just start digging it up; you weren't allowed to do that. I wanted to take a shovel and dig deep until I encountered an artifact or kitchen midden.

Another thing that presented a problem was Ford's cooking. He had brought up groceries for himself for that spring and summer, mostly canned goods and about 10 dozen eggs. All these items had been stored in the hospital basement to keep them from freezing, but he hadn't tried to preserve the eggs. When he cooked for us at the tent at shooting station, he didn't check the eggs before he cooked them and fried the rotten eggs with the good ones. I got deathly sick and for years after I couldn't eat eggs.

Ford excavated all summer. He accumulated a large amount of findings which he boxed up and shipped to New York on one of the cargo ships. He left us that summer to return to his work in New York and to continue his education.

Mr. Ford and I were sitting on the couch. He had a can of tobacco between his feet on the floor. Julia came down from making the beds upstairs and when she walked by she knocked the can over and Mr. Ford said, "Julia, pick up that can." She said, "No, no, Mr. Ford. No." Then he said, "Julia, you pick up that can of tobacco!" She got real mad and took a pair of scissors and threw them at him. She missed him, but after that I don't think Ford teased her anymore.

I encountered Ford eleven years later during World War II while I was flying fighters and bombers to Fairbanks for the Russians. While in Fairbanks at Eielson Air Force Base I was preparing to return to my home base of Great Falls, Montana when I observed a very tall man with a huge pack on his back. I knew immediately that it was

Ford. We exchanged greetings, very surprised to meet each other thus. "What are you doing here?" I asked. He was testing clothing for the government in cold weather conditions.

The next time I saw him was in 1958 at the University of Florida in Gainesville. He and his wife Ethyl entertained my wife and me in their home. He was then a curator for the museum at the University of Florida.

## THE LINDBERGHS VISIT

*In her memoir,* North to the Orient, *Ann Morrow Lindbergh recounted her arrival in Barrow. "This was Barrow, ten or twelve red roofs, numerous shacks and tents, a church steeple and—yes, there they were—the radio masts." Little did she know that a large reception, complete with Thanksgiving supper, had awaited her arrival for hours, an arrival delayed by ill weather. "I found myself running across the icy moss toward a lighted frame house. My hostess, the doctor's wife was leading me. I stamped my numb feet of the wooden steps of her home as she pushed open the door. The warmth of that kitchen fire, the brightness of gas lamps, and a delicious smell of sweet potatoes and freshly baked muffins poured our around me and drew me in."* (Lindbergh 1935:99)

In 1931 a wire came to Dad and Mother from the National Board of Missions in New York stating that they were to be host and hostess to the Lindbergh's during a short stop for refueling. They were on a trip to the Orient and were flying by way of Alaska since it was the great circle route.

This was summertime when the supply ships were bringing in our food stuff and supplies for a whole year, but many ships en route to the Arctic were stalled many miles down coast by the Arctic ice pack. We had some canned goods left but we were running low. However, the

*Fred Hopson, Charles Lindbergh, Ann Lindbergh, and me. Mrs. Lindbergh is wearing my mother's Arctic Squirrel skin coat.*

yearly house cleaning had been finished and it did not take long to get everything presentable.

Wireless operator Stanley Morgan, guided the Lindberghs into our village. The Colonel flew low over the lagoon twice before he made a perfect landing and taxied to where a small group of natives and whites greeted them quietly with many smiles and one big YA! YA! by the Eskimo. There was no crowding upon them as in other places. Two or three white and native men went close to the beach to be of any help. I had never seen a plane land on water before. It was quite a thrill. It took a good thirty minutes to anchor and tie up that plane. It was backed onto the beach with the nose pointing out.

Lindbergh got out first, then helped Mrs. Lindbergh out. The men on the beach helped her across the pontoons and onto the beach where she waited for her husband. Lindbergh threw a rope ashore and Lee Suvlu made it fast to a piece of driftwood buried in the sand with a bowline hitch. When Lindbergh came ashore he examined the tie down carefully, was pleased with it and that made Lee smile.

They all climbed the steep bank to the shore where the crowd waited. My mother greeted Mrs. Lindbergh first and then introduced her to Mrs. Morgan. The rest of the introductions were made by Father.

It was midnight when they arrived. We all walked up to the manse where Mother had had dinner waiting for a long, long time. Mother made them a goose dinner the first night and a reindeer dinner another night. We had no potatoes and had run out of canned peas and corn, but with Mother's homemade bread and biscuits the fare was suitable. Although it was still daylight outside, we let them go to bed at 3 a.m.

Breakfast was served to them on a tray at 9 a.m. that morning. They were told to make themselves at home and that my mother and father would be holding clinic at the hospital until 10:30.

During their visit I hitched up my team to Dad's sled and took them for a ride across the tundra, but it was slow going because there was no snow. We took a walk on the arctic ice pack and out on some ice bergs that were grounded on the beach. They visited Eskimo homes and were given gifts by the Eskimo. Pictures were taken and they visited Charlie Brower's trading post.

They attended church on Sunday and, on Sunday evening, Lindbergh spoke through an interpreter to the natives at church.

They indicated an interest in the meat cellar where it was -40 degrees so I was asked to take them down. Mother bundled them up in furs, Mrs. Lindbergh wearing my mother's fur coat and the Colonel wearing a fur-lined coat of Dad's. In an act of frivolity Colonel Lindbergh brushed some of the hoar frost—ice crystals that formed on the ceiling of the cellar—onto Mrs. Lindbergh's head. She turned around and hit him in a playful manner.

While visiting the hospital Mrs. Lindbergh even showed the Eskimo how to dance the Charleston. They were the most delightful young people anyone could wish to meet.

Every spare minute the colonel had he was reading Knud Rasmussen's book on his Fifth Thule Expedition in the Arctic which he found one morning in Dad's library.

While Mother was preparing her famous pancakes one morning, she saw through the open door way the Colonel taking down a book from Dad's library, writing something in it and putting it back. It was years later that by chance I opened up his book and found this written on the fly leaf, "to David Greist, Pt. Barrow, Alaska 1931 Charles A. Lindbergh."

One evening at the manse Colonel Lindbergh asked me and Beverly Morgan, who was ten, if we could stand on our heads. We said that we could not and he proceeded to take a pillow off of the couch and stand on his head with his feet against the wall. The next trick he showed us was how to chew two ends of a string together. I have performed that trick for hundreds of kids since then. It is one of the best tricks I have ever seen.

I asked Colonel Lindbergh what he would do if he knew they were going to crash. He said, "I would jump." "What about Mrs. Lindbergh," I asked. "If she wouldn't jump, I would throw her out," he replied.

Prior to their departure the Colonel spread his maps on the living room floor and spent quite a while studying them. I was curious and asked why. "David," he said, "eighty percent of flying is done on the floor, preparing for the trip. The other twenty percent is flying."

The Lindberghs stayed with us for three or four days. The USRC Northland was ice bound several miles down the coast with Lindy's gasoline, unable to reach Barrow. Being anxious to continue his journey, my father offered Lindbergh a supply of Stanov aviation fuel we had in our oil house.[55] He borrowed several 5 gallon cans of Stanov fuel to be replaced by his coming on the supply ship. With

Lindbergh on top of the wing, we boys carried the cans to him and he poured it into his tanks with the use of a large funnel.

As we all walked down to the lagoon for their takeoff, Colonel Lindbergh took my father aside and presented him with two checks, one to buy chairs for the church and the other to wire the manse and church for electric lights from the generators located in the hospital basement.

Three days later, when the *Northland* arrived, we learned that he had circled the ship twice where she was blocked by the Arctic ice pack before proceeding.

*Lindbergh's visit attracted wide attention. Newsreel footage was purchased from Barrow residents and shown in movie houses across the country. Photographs taken on the occasion continue to be cherished by Barrow residents and others such as David.*

## ROGERS & POST

*No discussion of notable visitors can be complete without mention of the crash of Wiley Post and Will Rogers near by at Walakpa. This one event and the coverage that it drew placed the North Slope of Alaska in the American consciousness as never before. The loss of such a national hero, as was Rogers at the time, in such a remote and unknown place attached an additional air of mystery and foreboding upon Barrow and the outlying area.*

Will Rogers, entertainer and writer, and Wiley Post, journalist and pilot, crashed at Walakpa, near Barrow, on August 15, 1935 at approximately 8:18 p.m.

Walakpa is a small lagoon 15 miles south of Barrow on the coast. It was used for corralling and counting reindeer herds and also was the site where seal hunters camped on the bluffs overlooking the Arctic Ocean. The lagoon is shallow and about 100 yards in length.

Rogers joked with Claire Okpeaha and his family who were camped in the area after they landed at Walakpa and gave them chewing gum while Post checked on the engine and its oil level.

They then both got into the plane and Post started the engine. He taxied to the far end of the lagoon and began his take off. Fifty feet from the water he began a left bank when the engine failed and the plane continued turning and diving into the lagoon. A wing was torn off and, upon impact, the engine was driven back into the cabin, crushing both men who reportedly died instantly. According to my father the attending physician, "I found water in their lungs thus indicating that they were killed instantly and were drowned. Both men's limbs were broken and both suffered severe head wounds."

Rescue natives extracted Rogers' body from the rear of the cabin. The plane had to be torn apart to extract Post's body which took the full impact of the engine. His wristwatch stopped at 8:18 p.m., when, in the Arctic, it was still daylight.

Post's plane was a Lockheed Orion. Post had wanted a larger wing so the wing from a Lockheed Sirus was installed, meant to give better lift off a short field during take-offs, especially on snow or water. The plane was bright red, 28 feet long with a wing span of 43 feet. It carried 220 gallons of fuel for a journey of 1,500 miles. The engine was a Wasp 550 hp geared supercharged. The prop was a three bladed controllable pitched Hamilton.

The plane was nose-heavy and on each take off Rogers had to get back as far as he could in the small cabin.

The wings and fuselage were purchased but Lockheed would not give its stamps of approval because the plane was made of various parts. Although air-worthy it incorporated different engineering designs.

*Following the crash, Dr. Greist and others prepared the bodies. Rogers, Post and parts of the plane were shipped south to California and Oklahoma. Several pieces of the plane remain in Barrow today.*

# CHAPTER EIGHT
# TRAVEL ON THE SEAS

*P* *rior to the advent of air flight, transport into the Arctic of people and cargo was a slow seasonal process, always full of risk in the form of floating ice and threatening weather. Although there were privately owned merchant ships, there were also service ships owned by the government that sailed the seas around the fledgling territory. The Bureau of Education owned ships which serviced the schools in the state and agents for the Office of Indian Affairs. These ships, such as the* Boxer *and* Northstar, *brought school supplies, while mission supplies arrived on merchant ships, such as the* Patterson *and* CS Holmes.

## REVENUE CUTTERS

*The United States Revenue Cutters were a branch of Coast Guard service that provided myriad travel, medical, dental, and legal services to visitors and residents of the Alaska territory. The ships' crews enforced the law, patrolling for illegal shipments of alcohol along the coast and keeping the general peace. Ships such as the* USRC Bear, *which transported the Greists back to Barrow after their long furlough in the 1920s, enabled doctors, scientists and others to travel about the territory.*

*These ships also kept an eye on the government's interests. Officers sailing on these vessels were charged with evaluating Alaska's natural and human resources and with resolving criminal problems. They served as the police and jail where marshals were not readily accessible and could ship prisoners out of communities if necessary.*

The Coast Guard was transporting people up in the Arctic. There you don't turn anybody down even if you're a battleship or something. They always carried people up and down the coast. It was a ship of many many activities and duties. They served as the law in the Arctic for many years. If someone was accused of shooting somebody else then a trial was held on the Coast Guard cutter and it was decided what to do with him. I don't know whether they performed marriages or not, but they were the law for many years. They also rescued ships that were caught in the ice if they possibly could.

Every Coast Guard cutter also had a doctor who would have treated people and some of them had a dentist too, like Dr. Waugh. If not a doctor, they had a medical technician. They were trained for all kinds of things except appendectomies and things like that, although I guess they could perform those too if they had to.

As long as the ship was right there its crew could come ashore everyday, maybe four or five days. A ship would anchor until all the cargo was ashore. If the ice started to come in, they would high-tail it around the point or someplace until the ice went out again and then they'd come back and continue their unloading. They would work day and night to unload that ship because of the ice. That ice was such a treacherous thing.

### The MS Patterson

The Motorship Patterson out of San Francisco was a two-masted sailing and motor ship used extensively for carrying freight and barter goods to the Arctic each summer to trade for furs at various villages along the coast. She was under the command of Captain C.T. Pedersen who had been sailing into the Arctic for some 40 years and had never lost a ship. From the late 1890s through the early 1920s he commanded a ship called the *Herman.*

The Patterson. *We were tied up to the ice pack for 15 days, unable to sail forward. Note the crows nest on the aft mast.*

The *Patterson* was 170 feet long with a 17-foot beam; her bow was covered with steel plates for protection against ice. Her engine was a diesel Fairbanks Moose 6 cylinder and, at 600 RPM, was capable of moving her through the water at 8 knots. With full sails she made about 10 to 11 knots.

The *Patterson* sailed into the Arctic each summer, leaving San Francisco in early June and reaching Dutch Harbor in the Aleutians in 21 days. There they filled the fuel tanks with diesel for the last time before entering the Arctic.

In August of 1930 I was sent to Santa Paula, California for my first year of high school. There I lived with my older brother, Elwood, and his family. The following June, being terribly homesick, I wasted no time in contacting Captain Pedersen and asking him for a berth to Barrow. "Yes," he said, "you can sign on as the cook's helper, $35 a month."

The summer of 1931 should be designated by ship masters who sailed the Arctic as one of the most perilous of their experiences. The arctic ice pack broke up very late, much more so than usual, and then, because of erratic currents and contrary winds, its vast field menaced all shipping for long weeks.

From Dutch Harbor we sailed across the Bering Sea past St. Lawrence Island to Nome, where we took on parcel post and mail which had accumulated there for several months. Upon entering the Bering Strait between Cape Prince of Wales on the Alaska Side and East Cape Siberia we encountered the first ice. We dodged ice, fought ice, blasted ourselves free repeatedly with dynamite and gunpowder and, for many days, slowly and painfully worked our passage through menacing ice fields toward the North.

One of the methods of cracking the ice field was by using black gunpowder that came in 5-pound cans. I would knock a hole into the can's top with a screw driver; insert a 2-foot fuse into the can and seal it with Fels Naptha yellow soap. The gun powder was then lashed to a long 2 x 4. One of us would light the fuse and two other fellows would thrust the can as far under the ice as they could and then we would run away a short distance and wait for the explosion. If we cracked the ice, we retrieved what was left of the two by four, climbed aboard the ship and Captain Pedersen would then order full speed ahead. The ship's bow would run up onto the ice and the weight of the ship would widen the crack. On several occasions we did this procedure all day long and the ship moved perhaps the distance of one mile.

At Icy Cape, some 150 miles south of Barrow, we were confronted by an immense ice field 10 feet thick which offered no advance, no avenue of forward progress. The next day another pan of ice, apparently unlimited in extent, came upon us from the stern and we found ourselves imprisoned within a field 10 miles long by as many broad. We lay fully a half a mile from open water, but we were utterly helpless and powerless against that ice. The ice was crushing, grinding, growling like an angry, enraged animal, seeking to annihilate us.

For 15 days we lay imprisoned in the ice some 2 miles off shore. In great numbers, natives from Wainwright camped on the beach evidently believing us to be doomed, apparently waiting expectantly for the *Patterson* to be crushed and abandoned; thus they would loot and gain the spoils of our doomed ship. During this time we were able to walk from ship to beach upon heavy ice, at will.

Our splendid captain had lost much sleep and eaten little. Many hours he spent in the "crow's nest" atop the highest mast searching with binoculars for any possible break in the ice or possible leads. As the cook's helper one of my duties was to climb the rigging to the "crow's nest" several times a day with a thermos of hot coffee and sandwiches. Often the captain would invite me to get into the "nest" and he would take time to point out the different types of ice fields to me. To a 14 year-old this was quite a treat. The US Revenue Cutter Northland had been advised of our situation. She said she would stand by to assist if the ice opened up sufficiently for an approach to our doomed ship.

On the 16th day the wind changed to the northeast and in a matter of hours that vast ice field opened up and we escaped to the northward toward Barrow, arriving off of my hometown on August 10th. After a very brief anchorage, Captain Pedersen hastened on around Barrow to safer waters and on eastward to Hershel Island on the Canadian side of Demarcation Point.

I left the ship at Barrow to stay with my parents for at least two or three weeks. When the *Patterson* returned from the east I got aboard for the lonely trip back to the States and back to school. Oh, how I hated to go back.

Sailing on the *Patterson* was a means of getting home. I sailed her three summers and when I arrived at Barrow, Captain Pederson would load me down with fresh eggs, apples, and oranges and, of course, all the first class mail for Barrow. Captain Pederson enabled me a chance to get home without buying a ticket, which I didn't expect.

On one of the times I was going home from school, his son, who was three or four years older than I, and I were playing catch ball on the deck just for something to do while we were going through the ice and the ball went overboard onto the ice. Captain Pederson was up in the crow's nest and he stopped the ship, backed it up and let us get our ball. He must have been looking down and watching us. He was quite a fella. Once when Captain Pederson was delivering a whole bunch of chairs to someone up the coast from Point Barrow and they had to be painted red, his son and I painted them red while crossing the ocean. We got them all done.

During my time on the ship I also learned alot about sailing and steering ships. Keep your eye on the front mast and on that front star—just keep your mast on that star and that's your compass. The captain also taught me not to make radical moves at the wheel. That helped me when I flew airplanes—if you go up 500 feet and just wait a few seconds, you'll lose 500 feet.

When I first started steering the *Patterson,* Captain Pederson was above me, watching. He walked to the stern to see what kind of wake we were making and then came back up to the front. He said, "David, I don't mind you writing your name, but don't go back to dot the I."

On one occasion when I was working as the cook's assistant, I had to take Captain Pederson sandwiches in the crow's nest. Soon after reaching the deck from making my delivery, I heard, "David, there is no butter on my sandwich." So I climbed the rigging to the nest and retrieved the sandwich. After that I never forgot the butter.

Mrs. Pederson was supposed to be a nurse at Barrow, but when she got there she found the missionary doctor was so sick that she turned around and took him back to the States. She later fell in love with Captain Pederson and married him.

Captain Pedersen retired from Arctic sailing in 1955. In 1958 while I was training to fly jets for the Air Force in Merced, California, Alicia, the children and I went to visit Captain and Mrs. Pedersen at their home in San Francisco. This was the last time we ever saw them alive. Some three months later two convicts escaped from prison and, as fate would have it, they found refuge in a shed behind Captain Pederson's home in San Francisco. They stayed in the shed till dark and then they broke into the Pedersons' house; probably to secure money or a car. The 90 year old captain fought them off as best he could, but they beat him unconscious and then attacked his wife. To make a long story short, Captain Pedersen died from his injuries and Mrs. Pedersen was confined to a mental institution where she died three years later. Both men were caught and are still in prison for double murder. Such a waste. Such a sad end to a very colorful career.

## GHOST SHIP OF THE ARCTIC: THE *Baychimo*

*The window for sailing through arctic water is very small and a wrong decision made by a captain to leave too late or stay too long could be disastrous. Shipwrecks were not an uncommon occurrence in the Arctic. Inexperienced captains or unpredictable weather could lead ships to be stranded, surrounded by ice or sunk after being struck by ice too sharp and too forceful.*

*When ships were stranded they sometimes had to be abandoned, left to the will of the sea. In those cases, every effort was made to get all hands off the ship, over the ice, and on to shore where they would find shelter or build a camp if far from a village. The men would attempt to contact their superiors for rescue and then take what they needed from the ship to survive. All else—merchandise, construction materials, and all—would be cast off with the ship. If a ship maintained its integrity and continued to float with the ice,*

The Baychimo, *the ghost ship of the North. Ira Rank's* Trader *is in the background.*

*everyone who happened upon it would investigate and salvage whatever could be had.*

Every summer several supply ships would sail through the Bering Strait into the Arctic to replenish coal, lumber, gasoline, kerosene, and food stuffs for the many small settlements and villages along the coast. Captain Pederson and the MS Patterson were for many years the first into the Arctic. He thus was able to get first choice of all the skins and furs from the natives along the coast waiting to do trade with the pelts they had saved from the previous trapping season.

I sailed with the *Patterson* several times and I would stand by in the captain's cabin where Captain Pederson was receiving furs from the natives. He would hold up a white fox, blow on the fur, shake it out and then say, "Sixty dollars." This was, of course, in trade; no cash was exchanged. Then the Eskimo could say, "I want 30-30 rifle and plenty ammunition." His son or I would run to the hold, get a rifle and several boxes of ammunition to make up the sixty dollars. It went on like that all day. Some of the natives would have twenty-five or thirty foxes to trade. They would end up with a lot of merchandise. Then they would load everything into their umiaks, go ashore and we would sail on to the next village.

The *Baychimo* was a supply ship owned by the Hudson Bay Company of Vancouver, Canada and she also made the journey each year. Her main assignment was to supply the Hudson Bay trading post at Hershel Island far to the eastward on the Canadian side of Demarcation Point. One year, however, she waited too long to make her return to the south. As she passed Barrow she encountered salt water slush which got thicker as she sailed toward Wainwright. At Peard Bay and the Sea Horse Islands[56], 40 miles north of Wainwright, the ship's engine[57] could not push her through the thick slushy ice which was then 6 to 10 inches thick. She was caught and the slush began to freeze around her.

The captain realized the situation was hopeless, so the crew left the ship and went ashore. Trading ships carried everything imaginable. There was enough lumber on board to build a large one-room shelter on the beach, complete with range, bunks for the men, and all furnishings to make them comfortable. An engine from one of the two launches was set up to turn a generator for electric lights. They were secure and warm, ready for the coming winter and their ship was frozen fast. All water had been drained from her pipes and engines. She had been "put to bed for the winter." One night in November a terrible blizzard developed; for two days no one ventured out from the shelter. On the third day the crewmen left the shelter and looked out to sea. The *Baychimo* was gone. Their beloved ship, frozen in the ice, had taken flight. They made sure it did not sink. After three weeks of housekeeping and routine existence the Canadians, having been wired of the crew's predicament from Wainwright, sent planes to take the crew back to Canada. Some believed that this was the end of the story... but not so.

Later that winter the *Baychimo* was sighted off Wainwright. The natives went out to her and climbed aboard, helping themselves to any supplies they found. One native found a wooden keg of sweet pickles in brine. Boy, did they enjoy those! Just as they had quickly collected their booty, the natives hurriedly left her and returned to their village. The *Baychimo* was moving on her ice floe.

That summer in August, a small trading ship called the *Trader* from Nome captained by Ira Rank saw the ghost ship far out to sea and pushed up on thick ice. They boarded her and helped themselves to anything they wanted and pictures were taken of her.

The next year the village of Barrow awakened one morning to see the *Baychimo* off shore on top of her ice floe as though to say, "Come on, I have plenty to spare." Many Eskimo went aboard and came back loaded down with all kinds of merchandise. They found a square box with a handle on it and inside was some kind of instrument. They didn't know what it was so they took it ashore and gave it to Mr. Morgan, thinking it was some kind of communication device. We later found out it was a Bausch and Lomb microscope.[58]

The next morning the *Baychimo* was gone.

The following summer I was on the *Patterson* en route to Barrow from the states when, in the distance, we saw a ship. Before we realized who she was, Captain Pederson said, "No ship has ever beaten me into the Arctic. Find out who she is." I climbed into the crows nest and, with a pair of binoculars, I could tell by the orange stripe around her smoke stack that it was the *Baychimo*.[59] I called down to the Captain on the bridge, "It's the *Baychimo,* sir!" "Well I feel better now," said Captain Pederson. He would not, however, take precious time to sail out to her and let us go aboard. I wanted to go aboard so badly.

During her last sighting to the eastward, a Canadian who had served on her, O.D. Morris[60], went aboard and he knew where a special store room was that no one else had ever found. In that room was over $10,000 worth of fox skins. He brought them ashore and the insurance company from Canada paid him a goodly sum for them.

That was the last time anyone saw the ghost ship. This all happened in the early 1930s. In 1936 I received a letter from a Miss Isabel Hutchinson of Scotland, a writer who had visited Barrow in 1931. She reported that a Canadian ship had sighted the *Baychimo* and that the ghost ship was still floating securely on her ice floe.

*Dr. Greist reported in* The Northern Cross, *"there was salvaged some 1,400 fox skins, which are in Barrow, being held for shipment. Some are very fine, and some not so good, but on the whole the $35,000 worth of fur is a sight to make any woman wink her eyes in delight and wish for a few."* (Greist 8/1932:20)

*In November of 1932 following the* Baychimo *'s next appearance in the Arctic, Dr. Greist reported, "Boys went out over the ice at great peril, secured some various articles from her, and had great difficulty in returning. Then without warning, she left again, and has not been seen since."* (Greist 11/1932:45)

## THE ARCTIC

In the whaling days of the 1800s, whalers would leave Boston, sail around the Cape of Good Hope and north past South America and North America into the Arctic where they stayed two or three years or until their ship was full of whale oil. As many as 200 sailing ships perished in the Arctic since the 1800s. Some of their skeletons are still found along the coast. Sailing into the Arctic Ocean each summer was probably the most dangerous venture for a ship anywhere in the world. Treacherous winds, currents and the ever-changing ice packing a tremendous force could crush a ship like an egg shell or raise it above the ice, high and dry.

My story of the *Baychimo* illustrates this. She was thrust up high on the ice and was observed by natives up and

The Artic *is sinking. Natives from Barrow are permitted to salvage anything on board.*

down the coast for at least three years as the pack carried her back and forth. I even saw her myself in 1932 from the crows nest of the *Patterson* using Captain Pederson's binoculars. I could plainly see the orange band around her black smoke stack. She was surrounded by solid ice and we could not approach within walking distance so we sailed on. After 1932 she was never seen again.

The *Arctic* was a four masted sailing ship out of San Francisco, carrying freight and trading goods into the Arctic at Alaska. In 1924 after unloading freight at Barrow she was the last ship to sail south and just ahead of the incoming ice pack. She waited too long and fifteen miles down the coast from Barrow she became surrounded by the ice where she was held fast. She was a wooden ship and soon the pressure of the ice opened up seams in her bottom and she began taking on water. The crew abandoned ship and walked a mile over the ice with their belongings to shore.

The natives of Barrow, including this writer, walked the fifteen miles to where she was slowly sinking. The Captain allowed them to salvage anything of value for themselves. Diving apparatus was unheard of at this time.

No one could dive into the cargo hold in that freezing salt ice water, so with grappling hooks everyone began pulling all kinds of stuff from that ship; sacks of sugar, flour, rice, and coal. Someone even hooked onto a sewing machine. While this was going on some of the natives salvaged the ropes and chains and canvas from the sails that were on deck. One native hacked out a port hole. One fellow hooked a box of rifles and he later gave one to Dad. It was a .44-40 brand new Winchester carbine which I used for several years in hunting at Barrow.[61]

As the cargo hold filled up with water, the ship began settling into the ocean and finally all had to leave her. As we gathered together several yards from the ship she slowly went down. It was such a sad sight to see such a beautiful ship disappear. The last thing we saw were her four masts going down.

## DR. GREIST LOST AT SEA

*Travel on sea ice was never a sure thing. Although seemingly locked fast to the land, the current beneath it could cause the ice to shift in ways that gave no warning and could have cataclysmic results. If a fissure were to open in a field of ice and a traveler were to be on the sea side of the lead, they could be lost out to sea unless able to cross the swiftly widening or closing fissures by boat.*

During our seventeen years at Barrow, Dad visited villages up and down the coast, ministering to the sick, performing marriages, preaching the gospel, and burying the dead of both whites and natives.

Wainwright is three days' travel in winter with a good team and Dad always stayed at Jim Allen's trading post. Dad made one particular trip in early spring, when the snow on the ice pack was beginning to melt, making travel slow.

After 4 days at Wainwright, Dad, Ned Nusunginya his driver and their eleven dog team started back. On the second day they made camp on the ice just a few miles north of Sea Horse Islands. During the night a northeaster sprung up and when they awoke the next morning they were cut off from shore and were on an ice slab half the size of a city block with the Arctic Ocean on all four sides. There was no way they could reach shore. This slab of ice had broken away from the shore ice which was grounded. There was little to do but walk back and forth on the ice, feed the dogs and pray. At their noon meal, Dad read the 91st Psalm to Ned and in his prayer he indicated to God that he was accepting the promises put forth in the 91st Psalm.

Near Barrow, younger herders were tending to their reindeer. The natives of Barrow kept their reindeer in a herd of about 2,000 head far inland from Barrow where the deer could forage for moss, their primary source of food. Twice a year, in the fall and the spring, the herd was brought into Barrow for butchering. To feed the village of 300 natives, 100 male reindeer were separated from the herd for meat. The skins were used for clothing, the muscle from the back was dried and torn into sinew thread with which the women sewed the skins together. When the butchering ended the herders took the herd back inland to grazing ground. The herders were young, single men from the village who stayed with the herd day and night. The young men of Barrow in their late teens and early twenties took turns in this assignment.

Ten miles inland from Barrow the herd had quietly settled down. In their tents, the boys were talking. "We are tired of eating reindeer meat. Tomorrow let's take the herd southwest toward the coast and in a day or two we will leave the herd 6 miles from the coast and two of us go to the coast and hunt seal." This was 4 days before Dad left Wainwright.

It took two and a half days to reach a suitable grazing area. While two herders watched the herd, Benjamin and Clyde took 30-30 rifles and headed for the coast. Sitting on the bluff overlooking the ice-filled ocean, Benjamin was using his brass telescope to look over the icebergs for seal. Suddenly he stopped and refocused the eyepiece. "Clyde," he said in Eskimo, "tell me what you see over there." Clyde took the telescope. "That is our missionary, Dr. Greist, and Ned. They are in bad trouble." Clyde, the youngest, decided to run to Barrow for help, leaving Benjamin to watch Dad and Ned.

After running three miles Clyde came to the mouth of a river which, several miles inland, was a small stream only 6 feet across. At this stage it was a fast moving stream 50 yards wide. What to do? He sat on the bank overlooking the river to the west and it was then that he smelled wood smoke. He walked over to the bank overlooking the ocean and there on the beach was a white tent, a skin boat pulled up on the beach and smoke coming out of the chimney of the tent. He ran down the bank and found a woman in the tent. Her two sons were down the beach hunting. Clyde told about the missionary. She, in turn, fired a rifle twice into the air—the signal to call the boys home. The three men launched the skin *umiak* and the boys picked their way through floating ice bergs. Nearly 6 hours later they reached the ice floe that my father was on. His sled, the eleven dogs and Ned were all loaded into the boat and paddled back to the fish camp by the river.

The Eskimo woman, anticipating their return, had made duck soup, sourdough bread and hot tea. Dad and Ned were welcomed with bear hugs from the Eskimo woman. She stripped both men down, wrapped them up in reindeer skins and fed them. The next day the woman, the three boys, Dad, Ned and all of the dogs were paddled to Barrow. Dad always claimed that the rescue was the answer to prayer and the providence of God.

## CHAPTER TEN
# AFTER THE COLD

*Although few who have lived in the shadow of Alaska's grandeur ever truly leave the state, the journey does sometimes come to an end. David Greist's childhood journey finished at the leaving of his parents from their tour as missionaries. Dr. and Mrs. Greist left the Arctic to return to an easier life in Indiana; David was continuing his education outside. Although he did make several trips back to serve his country, visit with friends and introduce his wife, he never again put down stakes and set up camp in any permanent fashion.*

*In 1938 David finished his secondary education at Stony Brook School for Boys and enrolled in Hanover University at Hanover, Indiana. There he earned his BA and met his first wife, Alicia. After graduating university in 1941, David entered the U. S. Army Air Corps, graduating as a pilot in 1942.*

*Late in World War II, David flew B-17's and B-24's over China. Following World War II, he was a flight commander over Canada and Alaska and lead flights to deliver aircraft to Russia. Stationed in California, he joined jet training in 1959. He was later assigned to Oklahoma where he assisted the FAA in qualifying pilots in jet flight. In 1964, he became the Commander of a 400 man, 15 plane K-135 squadron while assigned to McCoy Air Force base, Orlando, Florida. When all was said and done, he enjoyed a 24-year military career, flying 26 different planes for the Navy and Air Force. He retired from the Air Force in 1966.*

*While in the military, David attended Vanderbilt University, Southwestern State College (Oklahoma) and Rollins College (Florida), where he earned his Master's degree. Following his military career, David became a science teacher at the middle school level, deciding to follow Alicia's educational trail in reciprocation for her vigilant subscription to military life while raising their three children. After 25 years in education, he retired in to enjoy life in Florida and engage in real estate sales.*

*Today David is living well in Florida with his second wife, Rose. David still maintains contact with several of his childhood comrades in Barrow and has been back to visit several times, in 1968 and 1996. The Iñupiaq language still comes easily for him and the twinkle of Iñupiaq humor, instilled in him as a child, still glows brightly in the smile that accompanies his memories of Alaska.*

# NOTES

1. *Dr. Greist had wanted to be a missionary in a foreign field even as a boy. He turned down a medical appointment to Japan earlier in life and his first offer to go to Alaska several years earlier. The second time an offer came for an Alaskan appointment, he accepted it readily and immediately began studying for exams that allowed him to be ordained as a Presbyterian minister.*

2. *Previously married, both Henry and Mollie Greist had parented children years prior to meeting. Mollie's only other child, a son from her first marriage named James Ward (Buster) Butler, died of Pott's Disease—tubercular damage to the vertebrae which causes curvature of the spine—at the age of 12, mere months before David's birth.*

3. After this they were sent to Barrow, the farthest northern tip of Alaska well within the Arctic Circle and only 1,250 miles from the North Pole. Barrow was a village of 300 Eskimos, 12 whites, and 700 dogs.

4. I broke my arm on that trip, chasing a cat. All ships had cats, you know. I was chasing this cat and I chased him up the stairs and I chased him down the stairs and that's how I broke my arm. I'd never seen a cat before and my father set my arm for me.

5. Incidentally the boy's father took him up on the side of the mountain where the dead were buried by dropping them down between boulders. The father had his son stand near the crevice and shot him so that he fell into his own grave.

6. In all the years in Alaska nothing was ever stolen from our hospital and mission doors were never locked.

7. *Although subterranean sod houses were also in use, they had disappeared by 1926* (Greist 8/1932).

8. If someone had collected driftwood on the beach, they could leave their finds in a pile and no one would disturb them. If a native trapper found a fox in someone else's trap, he would not disturb it, knowing it belonged to another.

9. *Waste from the chemical toilets would be collected in barrels and placed outside to freeze. Once frozen it would be dumped in the ocean.*

10. After we left, the first government doctor arrived at Barrow drunk. The elders of the village arranged to have him delivered back on the ship and return to the States.

11. One could cross a stream in waterproof boots only to leave them on the other side, half buried in sand.

12. You can shoot at them from off of a boat, too. Then you spear them and pull them on board.

13. *Among the many jobs she had during her time in Barrow, Mollie collected biological specimens—eggs and bird carcasses— for museums in the lower 48. Although the current home of the specimens is uncertain, they were originally shipped to museums in the lower 48, including Hanover College, Hanover, Indiana.*

14. *Baleen is the horn-like substance that hangs in the mouths of toothless whales and serves to strain food from the water. It exists as long, thin, triangular sheets which lie closely together, being connected by a type of gum at one end. It ranges in color from dark off-white to black and possesses strands of hair-like baleen over one, long edge of each plate which serves as strainer. In pre-contact times it was used as a fiber, cut into lashings and bucket handles and such. Today's it's greatest use is found in the tourist art market. It was often called whalebone by earlier travelers to the Arctic.*

15. *David would set traps as he traveled in a circle toward his first trap. He could then check his traps by traveling the loop he had created that lead back to camp, always arriving back at the same place he had started.*

16. Victor was a popular brand of steel trap then.

17. The meat, even when frozen, was kept separate from the rest of the load on the sled.

18. A Primus is a Swedish brass kerosene stove that burns a nice white flame. With alcohol you have to heat up a generator which converts the kerosene to a gas. There is a little orifice in the generator which would get plugged up and you had a very thin wire you'd push down in there to clear it out. When we didn't have one of those cleaning wires we'd take a whisker from one of the dogs and use that. It really did the trick.

19. When the ceiling of the snow house started to drip water I would take my hunting knife and cut off the icicle that was hanging down and that would stop the drip for a few minutes or until I turned off the heat.

20. Dogs will stay close to camp because the camp is where there is a food source. I seldom turned the dogs loose. In this situation with the blizzard the alternative would possibly have been a dog or dogs buried alive in snow.

21. The prevailing winds are from the northeast. Small snow drifts on the hard surface of a lake look like this:

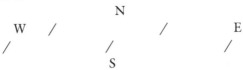

You can therefore cross them at any selected angle for the desired compass heading.

22. You do not allow two strange teams of dogs to fraternize or a fight will occur between the dogs possibly resulting in severe injury to some and even death. I still carry scars on my arms from dog bites, when I tried to stop a fight.

23. *In much of the Arctic literature, Ellnou is often referred to as Eleanor by members of the contemporary white culture. She became Jim Allen's wife after a very proper courtship in 1903. Her parents were from Kivalina, approximately 60 miles south of Point Hope on Alaska's northwest coast.*

24. Sally was the daughter of one of Knud Rasmussen's dogs. I mated Sally with Jim Allen's police dog and the results were two brown puppies named Sonny and Brownie.

25. We had the only group dog house. The only time they were forced to sleep in inclement weather was on the trail.

26. *In addition to Mr. and Mrs. Trindle, the other teachers employed during the Greists' time in Barrow included Mr. and Mrs. Nichols, Peter van der Steere, Mr. and Mrs. Daugherty, and Mr. and Mrs. Stowell. There were also Iñupiat teachers and teachers' aides, including Roy Ahmaogak, Percy Ipalook, Ethel Sage and Flossie George Connery.*

27. *Adults could also be creative in their pursuit if entertainment. The white men of Barrow fancied themselves cake bakers at one time, matching skills in weekly competition.*

28. We mostly listened to cowboy songs. "Red River Valley", "The Last Great Roundup", "Dying Cowgirl", "May I Sleep in Your Barn Tonight, Mister?", and "Home on the Range" were all popular. One year I ordered fifteen records from Sears in Seattle by COD. Mr. Brower was the postmaster and when they

came he didn't even collect from me. He just said, "David, here are your records." He, no doubt, paid the charges himself.

29. My mother even drew a cover for *The Northern Cross* on one occasion.

30. Sometimes a piece of blubber about 4 x 5 x 2" would burn for 30-60 minutes and give a real hot heat on a small stove. Dad said it was awfully hard on stove grates; they'd get red hot.

31. Some bowhead whales captured in the Arctic showed evidence of the prehistoric remains of legs. It is believed that whales can live to be 100. We caught whales in the Arctic that carried harpoons imbedded in their bodies from whaling ships out of Bedford, Massachusetts dated 1898.

There are a large variety of whales, the finback is the most common it reaches a length of 60 to 70 feet with flippers 5 or 6 feet long. The finback has baleen in its mouth and feeds on shrimp. The humpback has flippers nearly 14 feet long, baleen in the mouth and is found in the Arctic Ocean. The blue whale can reach a length of 100 feet and weigh as much as a 140 tons. This is the largest of all whales and is not found in the Arctic Ocean.

32. At Barrow while I was there, any white man could participate and go whaling in a whale boat with a crew. Not many teenagers went for there was school to attend and to sit out on the ice by an open lead day after day waiting and waiting and with very subdued talking—whales have a very keen sense of hearing—would have been boring.

*Today, the Marine Mammal Protection Act of 1972 prohibits Caucasian community members from killing whales and although some Barrow crews have white members helping on shore and at home, few if any allow them to participate in the boat crew to avoid speculation regarding individual responsibility for a whale's death.*

33. The frame is made of drift wood and covered with *ugruk* hide. Operated by paddles only, sometimes a sail to supplement the paddles. I have counted as many as twenty-two natives in an *umiak*. A very sturdy and popular boat.

34. These are no ordinary doughnuts, but Eskimo doughnuts—a type of fry bread made into sausage shapes and fried in seal oil over an oil stove.

35. Nalukataq *is preceded by* Apugauti, *the celebratory time earlier in the summer when the successful whaling crew boats were brought in from the ice of the spring whaling. With crew flags*

*flying above them, the successful boat is brought ashore, prayers of thanks are said. The crew serves all those who come out to greet them* mikigaq, *goose soup and Eskimo doughnuts.*

36. *At today's* nalukataq, *it is not uncommon for a crew member to jump on the bearded seal blanket (also called* nalukataq) *and throw bags full of candy to the crowd that stands around to watch.*

37. All white people participated in *nalukataq.* Very few whites, if any, would be tossed on the skin, however. I can remember Mother and Peter van der Steere dancing. I even began to dance when I was around 4 years of age.

38. They had married sisters in Indiana in 1890. Uncle Lew had two boys, Harold and Ray, and a daughter, Charlotte. Dad had three sons from this marriage, Wishard, Arnold, and Elwood. Dad was divorced from his wife in 1910, and married my mother in 1915.

39. This lumber was imported from the States. Small sleds in the absence of hickory used 2 x 6's or 2 x 8's. These were used by children sometimes with one or two dogs in harnesses pulling them. They were used in the winter for carrying objects too heavy to carry and were pulled by rope.

40. *By 1936, the Barrow herd numbered approximately 40,000.* (Greist 3/1936:47)

41. Charles Brower fathered a large family, some 15-18 children. All Brower girls became good cooks. To name a few, Sadie, Maria, Mary, Kate, and Jenny.

42. Why? I asked a friend of mine today (Orlando March 26, 1997) Roger Bristol, a fine master mechanic this question—"The engines in the '20s and '30s including the model "T" Ford were low combustion engines and once they heated up you could burn kerosene in them. They ran like a diesel. You can't do that with the modern engines which are high compression." Thanks Roger, Lee and I didn't know.

43. *Parcel post came only once each year on the ship in the summer.*

44. *The* Baychimo *was a ship that, having been wrecked on and frozen in the ice, floated around the Arctic for a period of time. Whenever it appeared on the horizon within site of a village, people would travel out to the ship and loot its contents.*

45. If I had fallen into the moving tread, I would have been pulled forward and crushed under the tractor. The treads had no fender to cover them or protect the driver.

46. Dad used several dog team drivers—Bert Panigeo, Roy Ahmaogak, Bud Hopson, Ned Nusunginya, and Lee Suvlu. They were men active in the church who spoke English well and could interpret for Dad when attending the sick or even interpret his sermons in other villages.

47. Eskimos learned to play the harmonica because they were in the mission boxes. Every Eskimo boy played a harmonica.

48. *Wishard was a half-brother from Dr. Greist's previous marriage who wrote the entire blueprints for the house. He was never able to go to Barrow to see the finished product.*

49. Wind, rain, and fog were adverse weather conditions we contended with. Temperatures were in the '50s and '60s.

50. I did not know of any white or Eskimo family that did not have a rifle or shot gun. In our hallway by the front door my father and I had rifles and shotguns on a gun rack, all loaded and ready to go. I knew Dad to stand on the front porch and shoot ducks, geese and plover.

51. Gasoline also came in 5 gallon cans, two to a box. The aviation fuel that Dad had in that oil house was Stanov gasoline from Standard Oil Co. and it was also in 5 gallon cans.

52. The tractor could pull two 16 foot sleds full of ice on one trip. This amount of ice would have taken a dog team 10-15 trips to accomplish. The native hauled fresh water by team in wooden barrels or empty 5 gallon gasoline cans from the lakes during the summer for drinking purposes. None of them had ice houses as I recall. The school teacher, our mission, Mr. Brower, and Sergeant Morgan the Army wireless operator all had ice houses.

53. Captain John Backland seldom left his ship to visit the village. However, one year he did come ashore to have dinner with my parents. The ice was no threat and he felt safe in coming ashore. At that time he presented me with a red wagon. That was in 1924 and I was 6 years old.

54. *Mollie Greist made note in the August 1932 issue of* The Northern Cross *that there remained "but two ancient Eskimo oil stoves in Barrow", adding that one of them would be shipped to the Smithsonian that summer along with two tons of "ancient curios." The Greists continued the tradition of exporting pieces of traditional material culture during their stay in Barrow.*

55. This was a warehouse which housed only kerosene and gasoline and Dad had several cases of Stanov aviation fuel, probably a Standard Oil product. It was high octane gasoline. Where Dad

got the fuel I don't know, unless it was left there for some bush pilot or even the explorers Amundsen or Rassmusen who had been to Barrow in the early 1920s.

56. There are no sea horses in the Arctic; I don't know why they were called that.

57. She was powered by a Fairbanks Morse diesel engine with six cylinders as big as wash tubs.

58. Mr. Morgan gave this instrument to my father after Dad performed an emergency appendectomy on Mr. Morgan's father while he visited Barrow. When my father returned to the states in 1936, he brought the instrument with him and presented it to his grandson, newly graduated from Stanford with an MD. Dr. Elwood Greist, Bud as we called him, still has this microscope from the *Baychimo*.

59. The smoke stack of the *Patterson* was all black. The *Baychimo*'s stack was black but had an orange stripe painted around it near the top. It was the only ship in the north that I knew of painted in that fashion and was quite recognizable

60. O. D. Morris was from Coronation Gulf, Northwest Territories, Canada and had served on the *Baychimo*. He and his family, daughters Charmaine and Cleo, lived in Fairbanks.

During World War II, I was in Fairbanks in 1944 delivering a fighter P-39 to the Russians. I found O. D. Morris's address in the phone book and drove out to his cabin, but no one was home. I left a note, but never heard from him again.

61. I also learned later that I could fire 410 shotgun shells in it. Our family still has this gun, my nephew Elwood Greist in California is presently its owner.

# WORKS OF RELEVANCE

Allen, Jim 1978 *A Whaler and Trader in the Arctic, 1895 to 1944.* Anchorage: Alaska Publishing Co.

Blackman, Margaret B. 1989 *Sadie Brower Neakok, an Inupiaq Woman.* Seattle: University of Washington Press.

Bodfish Sr., Waldo 1991 *Kusiq: an Eskimo Life History from the Arctic Coast of Alaska.* Fairbanks:University of Alaska Press.

Brower, Charles 1942 *Fifty Years Below Zero.* New York: Dodd, Mead and Co.

Greist, Henry W.
  1922 Letter to George F. Jenckes, May 9, 1922.
  1933 Letter to J. A. Ward, November 20, 1933.
  1955 "Seventeen Years With the Eskimo." Typescript. Dartmouth College Library, Stefansson Collection.

Greist, Henry W., and Mollie Ward Greist 1929-1936 *The Northern Cross.* n.p. January 1929 - August 1936.

Greist, Mollie Ward 1967 *Nursing Under the North Star.* Monticello, IN: White County Historical Society.

King, Irving H. 1996 *The Coast Guard Expands, 1865-1915.* Annapolis: Naval Institute Press.

Lee, Molly 1983 *Baleen Basketry of the North Alaskan Eskimo.* Barrow, AK: North Slope Borough Planning Department.

Lindbergh, Anne Morrow 1935 *North to the Orient.* New York: Harcourt, Brace and Co.